# Muntjac

# Muntjac

*A study of these small elusive*
*Asiatic deer which colonized an*
*English garden*

*by*

## Eileen A Soper

*Illustrated by the Author*
*and with a Foreword*
*by*
*Ernest G Neal, M.Sc., Ph.D.*

Longmans

LONGMANS, GREEN AND CO LTD
London and Harlow
Associated companies, branches and representatives
throughout the world

© Eileen A Soper 1969

First published 1969

SBN: 582 10143 3

Printed in Great Britain by
Lowe & Brydone (Printers) Ltd., London

# Contents

# Foreword

To most people the word Muntjac means very little—perhaps just the name of some foreign type of deer seen behind bars at one of the Zoos and quickly passed by. It is probably true that even the majority of naturalists have never seen one in the wild, yet ever since the Duke of Bedford brought them to Woburn at the beginning of the century they have spread over the neighbouring counties and unobtrusively carved out for themselves an important niche in the English countryside.

Muntjac are difficult to see because they are largely nocturnal in their behaviour and being so small of stature they can hide away in vegetation very successfully.

To study them it is difficult to find a focal point from which to start your observation. They have no earth or set like foxes or badgers which make the watching of these animals comparatively easy. They constantly change their resting places after the slightest disturbance; they make no special nest for their young which could be constantly watched, and chance meetings tell you little unless you are fortunate to catch sight of them before they see you— a most unlikely event. These are formidable difficulties to the naturalist who sets out to study Muntjac and they account, no doubt, for the scarcity of detailed knowledge about the life history and behaviour of these secretive creatures.

Eileen Soper has overcome many of these difficulties by making her large wild garden a very desirable source of food and cover for the deer—a safe oasis in a countryside largely hostile to the larger animals. Having attracted them she then set about the task of allowing them to tolerate her presence; this needed great patience and a sensitive appreciation of their way of life: but it was achieved, and this gave her the chance to observe their behaviour more successfully.

But knowledge gained in this way is often fragmentary and there are often long gaps between sightings. This is when tracking becomes a necessity and in this Eileen Soper is expert. She has the observant eye of the artist for minute details and the deductive mind of the detective. As a result her accounts are both detailed and of scientific value.

The story of these deer which she came to know so intimately is the result of watching over eight years. As she gained their toleration so her enthusiasm increased and her watching took place in all weathers often for prolonged periods. Gradually she was able to build up a picture of their comings and goings, some of their food preferences, the cycle of growth of the antlers and their shedding, their period of rut and the times when the fawns were born. This is a fine achievement and adds considerably to knowledge of Muntjac in the wild. Some of these things would not have been discovered unless the animals had been known as individuals, as unlike many deer there is considerable variation within the species regarding time of rut, period of birth and hence individual behaviour. It is this variation between individuals that has led to so much vagueness in the literature.

The charming illustrations add much to the value of this book as they not only bring delight, but show in a way that words alone cannot express the characteristic attitudes and behaviour of the individuals she portrays.

The book is not confined to the story of Muntjac, and the author's descriptions of the wild life which keep company with the deer make delightful digressions.

I am glad this book has been written. It will encourage others to go and do likewise. It shows what can be done without recourse to sophisticated scientific techniques, relying only on patient enquiry, persistent detailed observations, critical deductions and a sensitive awareness of animal needs. But it is not just a book for the naturalist; it will bring pleasure and refreshment to those who wish to turn aside for a few hours from the strains of modern life and get a glimpse of the pulsating life of the countryside which it is everyman's duty and privilege to conserve for future generations.

Ernest G Neal

# Preface

Muntjac deer have spread widely in the countryside since a number wandered from Woburn Park where they were introduced by the Duke of Bedford about sixty years ago. Shy and retiring in habit, they have since become established in many counties, as their small stature—they stand about twenty inches at the shoulder—enables them to travel unseen for long distances in the cover of herbage. Hertfordshire was one of the first counties to be colonised but it was not till 1961 that the deer came to our garden which, as a wild life sanctuary of long standing, offered an ideal habitat. This was originally created by my father, George Soper, whose work as an artist and Fellow of the Royal Society of Painter Etchers and Engravers is well known for its fine rendering of the English countryside. His pictures are a unique record of work on the land before the advent of modern machinery replaced the horse teams, the plough, the wagons, and other graceful implements of the farm. He was, too, a keen gardener and student of nature, and the habitat he designed has, through its natural form, proved attractive to a variety of wild life. His botanical interests were wide, and the garden soon contained a fine collection of plants, many of which were rare and difficult in cultivation. But through his knowledge and understanding of their needs they flourished with abandon, naturalising themselves in the semi-wild situation he devised.

The garden was created on the slope of a meadow overlooking a wide landscape of field and woodland, open to the south wind, to sunlight and changing skies. Shaped to the artist's vision, it lost little of the wild element, and the meadow was never entirely tamed. But in time, growing trees and shrubs changed its character: birds of the fields, which had nested there in the garden's early days, began to seek more open land, and to be replaced by those of woodland and hedgerow. As the years passed, the demise of certain species, which was occurring throughout most of Britain, also affected the garden population. Red-backed shrikes no longer nested in the thorn bushes, wrynecks and nightingales began to disappear, and of the smaller mammals the red squirrel was rarely seen, and the dormouse no longer a breeding species in the garden.

ix

Among the plants, which included many natives, for which my father had a deep affection, were a variety of species from the Far East. This area of the world has given a wealth of plant life to British gardens, and later the coming of Asiatic deer seemed a fitting acquisition, for unknowingly they had chosen a habitat rich in their own native flora. Chinese roses, clematis, diapelta, bamboo, magnolia, and other eastern shrubs gave shelter, with ground cover that included many plants of exotic origin. The deer found seclusion in the bamboo thickets, beneath mounds of spiny rose bushes and tangled clematis, and in winter evergreens and flowering shrubs, as *Hammamelis mollis* (one of the best China has given) *Chimonathus fragrans*, viburnums and many others helped to screen them from too inquisitive eyes.

My father did not live to see the coming of muntjac, and when he died my sister and I took over the responsibility of the garden and sanctuary. Our affections for plant and animal life were shared, but it was natural that my sister, who had inherited Father's skill in the garden, should find her chief interest in the plants, while mine was more definitely centered on wild life.

Before the deer came we had no large mammals on our land apart from visiting foxes, though the birds were a continual source of pleasure and study. Our father had been interested also in the wild life of the surrounding countryside, and I remember from childhood many a thrilling expedition or dawn watch in the outlying woods and fields. I continued this interest, and, eventually, finding a badgers' sett not far from home, began some intensive watching. I was at once under the badgers' spell, and for many years following went out night after night to the setts, watching the animals, studying their behaviour, and making sketches of them in the wild. From this my book, When Badgers Wake evolved.

Time brought further change to the garden, and the deer found overhanging thickets, lush herbage and shrubs mingled together, which gave welcome hiding places into which they could retreat, when they chose, from lawns and clearings.

We have always encouraged the birds, and in such a garden the choice of nesting sites is almost unlimited. But as a further inducement we added to the natural amenities by the erection of nesting boxes, and a wide variety of birds come to rear their broods undisturbed. Food and water are always available, either through nature's provision or our own in winter, and countless birds come to the feeding tables. Many are exceptionally tame, and robins, chaffinches, nuthatches and tits— even the long-tails—feed from the hand. They find their way into the house, going from room to room, and the studio has long been a part of their territory—an indoor shelf is a perfect nesting site for a robin, and the naturalist could scarcely find a more convenient subject.

In autumn the fruits of the garden are shared by deer and birds. Though the deer are very selective, there are few berried shrubs which do not attract a variety of birds, including redwings and fieldfares fluttering hungrily among the branches on the coldest days of winter. And the lure of the cone bearing trees brings cross-bills to feed in years of their irruption.

Various small mammals have always been established residents, having discovered early the attractions of the wilder parts of the garden, but unfortunately some species cannot be named as gardeners' friends. Voles have large appetites which seem at times insatiable, and they frequently choose, with the discretion of the connoisseur, the best plants in the garden. But the delinquence of some species is partly offset by the good work of others, as the shrews, hedgehogs and toads, which help to eliminate harmful grubs. Severe weather brings fox and hare from the fields, and sometimes in periods of drought a wandering badger in search of wasps' and wild bees' nests, which we find ravaged, though the badger, as my favourite mammal, is perhaps the most welcome of all.

The deer have no quarrel with any of these except the fox, whose visits I once looked forward to but now dread if there is a young fawn in the family. The garden offers a great variety of habitat to wild life, and it is here that my chief study of Chinese muntjac has been concentrated—the following chapters are a record of watching over a period of nearly eight years. Some of the deer's secrets I have shared, others perhaps they will always keep, as I hope they will find and keep environments wild as their own free spirits.

Eileen A Soper

# CHAPTER I

# Chasing Shadows

THE iron roof of the old pigsty flapped and clattered in the wind, and rats ran over my feet as I stood watching the dreary landscape outside. The last of the sunset light was dying; grey clouds were scudding across the December sky. Here in the decaying orchard, the haunt of didicots in search of anything that could be scrounged by night from the disused small holding, I had chosen to wait in the hope of seeing muntjac, diminutive Asiatic deer whose whereabouts were as uncertain as wind and weather, and whose shy disposition made them very difficult to observe.

All this now seems a long time ago—1959 and my first efforts to study their mystic ways; to piece together the happenings of their yearly cycle.

The only reward I had for my lone missions in that tangled waste was an occasional glimpse of muntjac, and from time to time the sound of their eerie barking in the darkness. Friends whose gardens adjoined the orchard were more fortunate, though the deer's appearances were always erratic. But my enthusiasm was renewed by the discovery of what appeared to be a deer's sanctuary in a near-by gravel pit. Their much trodden path led up to a tunnel through a huge mound of bramble at the top of a steep cutting, which doubtless concealed their hideout, and this seemed a promising place to watch. But even there I saw little of muntjac behaviour, and counted myself lucky if I saw deer at all. It was impossible to know where they might be at any given time. I found tracks and other signs over a wide area including woodland and heath, suggesting that their territory was extensive. Time for watching here was limited as this quiet unspoilt countryside was scheduled as the site of a coming motorway. Work began in 1960. It cut the deer's territory in half, and involved part of the gardens, the old orchard, and a vast amount of woodland and heath which had long been a local beauty spot. I continued watching but the evening quiet was shattered by the din of excavators working in the site till dark, and to add to the disturbance numbers of children came with their dogs from late afternoon till dusk, shouting through the woods, to watch the destruction. Surprisingly, at least some of the deer remained in the area, and continued to use what was left of their territory, but the chances of seeing them were so slight that I transferred my attention to an estate nearer home where deer were in residence. I had some interesting watching there, but they were very secretive, and my plans to compile a record of the muntjac's year seemed far off and illusory.

It was with these depressing thoughts in mind that I wandered into my own garden one February morning, and with the naturalist's habit glanced down at the wet mud for tracks. I expected no specific signs, but hoped that a wandering fox, badger, or hare had been through overnight. I stopped suddenly—at my feet, clear and indisputable, were the slots of a muntjac doe and her fawn!

The garden was at once a source of expectation and delight, for deer bring a sense of charm to any place they haunt, and the possibilities for watching were great. But on reflection I realised that this might prove to be just a passing visit arising from disturbance of their sanctuary in outlying woods.

Following the slots, I found that the deer had explored most of the garden, wandering along paths and through flower borders; into the wood and the water garden, where the doe had paused to pluck a mouthful of ivy, and here on the damp path the tiny slots of the fawn were deeper, more crisply cut, suggesting a sudden frolic; a moment of joy under the stars.

This, as later events were to show, was only a beginning. The hidden ways, dense shrubs and thickets of the garden offered shelter that was reassuring. A sense of freedom pervaded the tangled overgrown areas, welcoming to any animal in search of seclusion.

My first glimpse of the deer came in the afternoon, when unwittingly I sent her leaping from cover to disappear so completely that she might never have existed. But I planned to watch at sundown, and put up a step-ladder concealed among trees overlooking the bamboo thicket she had left. I hoped she had her fawn there in hiding and would return later. I was building my hopes on frail assumptions, but naturalists are by nature optimistic. I saw nothing of the deer that evening, or on several other attempts, and the possibility that they had gone elsewhere began reluctantly to dampen my ardour.

A step-ladder or the bough of a tree are not comfortable to stand on for any length of time, specially in winter, but watching at night or in the early morning, even if the hoped for animals fail to come, always has something to offer. The mystery of twilight, changing skies moonlit or at first light have rare beauty. Watching from the ladder I was often very close to birds as they came to roost in the trees beside me, and at dawn awoke to preen and sing. There is a unique quality in bird song at close quarters, when even the quietest notes are heard, and the full richness of song sounds loud and clear across the early light.

Deer are wayward creatures, and over an area of several acres the possibility of seeing them depends largely on chance. The use of a hide above ground-level helps to prevent their scenting the watcher, but it was not in this case infallible as they were inclined to approach from almost any direction. Down wind they could detect human scent from some distance, and the slightest sound was likely to alert them. There was too the disturbance of traffic in the lane, which they sometimes crossed to reach the garden; a car, cyclist or pedestrian might turn them back and delay their coming for hours. This was only one of the many evening hazards

when people were more often abroad than at dawn. The extent and volume of noise in a residential area by night is known perhaps only to the naturalist standing out-of-doors, waiting, listening, apprehensive of any interruption that will ruin the chances of success. But reward, when it came, was great, and worth much time and patience; much shivering in the February cold. The sudden appearance of the doe and her fawn brought a thrill comparable only to that experienced when a badger long-awaited emerges from the sett, or a fox cub trips silently across the moonlit grass—moments for which the dedicated are prepared to wait almost indefinitely.

Deer are never easy to watch in the wild. Their existence depends on acute perception of danger, and observation of any species is a challenge to the field naturalist. The smaller the deer the more difficult the task becomes, and muntjac have long perfected the art of avoiding contact with man.

Of the two species—Chinese muntjac, *Muntiacus reevesi* and Indian muntjac, *Muntiacus muntjak*—liberated years ago in Britain, the Chinese has been the more successful. None of the pure Indian version is thought now to be feral in the countryside. But earlier, crossing occurred between the two, and it is difficult to be sure whether the small deer one sees is in fact a Chinese muntjac or a hybrid, for numbers of these are also at large. For this reason most muntjac are cautiously described by naturalists as *Muntiacus spp.* I had this problem in the garden, but when later in my study of the deer one was found dead, I took the skull to the British Museum, where Mr Robert Hayman and I compared it with other specimens. We found no evidence to suggest that this was a hybrid, and

4

concluded that the deer of the garden were, at that time at least, pure *Muntiacus reevesi*.

In the past few people have seen deer in Britain, except in parks and zoological gardens, but since the introduction of foreign species the chances of encountering some have been greater. There are Japanese sika, *Cervus nippon nippon* in a number of counties, particularly in the south and west, also in parts of Scotland and Ireland. A few appear from time to time near my home, and when seen are usually reported as native red deer, to which they are of course related and bear a resemblance. Some Chinese water-deer, *Hydropotes inermis* (escaping from Woburn), have increased and become established in Bedfordshire, Herts. and Bucks. Other species, as chital or axis deer, of Indian origin, have with Indian muntjac, failed to survive in our climate.

The colonisation of the countryside by Chinese muntjac and their hybrids took place almost unnoticed, for the species is secretive by nature, and the deer small enough to remain hidden in the herbage, where with head held low, and shoulder height a mere eighteen to twenty inches they can travel a long way unseen. These retiring habits presented difficulties to the watcher in the garden, as elsewhere, particularly when the leaves unfolded. The deer could lie up all day unnoticed or creep along beneath the herbage secure from view; and to search for them meant disturbance, which I was anxious to avoid. If by chance they were driven from cover I never attempted to follow, as I hoped in this way to induce them to remain in or near the garden.

In summer the ground was rarely wet enough to register slots, but at gaps in the hedges used by deer, I put down sand, which I kept damp by watering. On this I found adult slots regularly, though there was no sign of the fawn that came earlier with the doe, and the deer had themselves reverted more or less to shadows haunting the wild parts of the garden. These offered close cover, and doubtless gave the deer a sense of security.

During the summer of that year I rarely saw them, but in autumn when the leaves blew off and the garden was more open, I began to encounter them again. One evening, as a result of careful stalking, I found myself almost face to face with a fine young buck. I came upon him suddenly, and no more than a dozen paces divided us, but he stood his ground staring at the scant bush which I felt gave me little cover. I remained rigid, crouched in an awkward position which soon threatened to become unbearable. Presently the buck, seeming reassured, began to browse from ivy at his feet, looking up occasionally to stare in my direction. This continued for about ten minutes, with the deer alternately feeding and watching. Suddenly he stamped a foot, rubbed his head nonchalantly along his side, and trotted away, tail up, showing his white target—probably a sign that he had, after all, sensed my intrusion.

Following this meeting with the buck, his slots were found in the garden daily, and he seemed to have adopted it as part of his territory. But it was not till the first snow of winter that I began to see him frequently. Then, too, I could follow his overnight wandering by clearly defined slots. I saw where he had walked by the food put out for him; where he had taken the preferred holly or ivy from the hedge. In these hungry days any plant above the snow line was vulnerable, and unfortunately the deer had no gardening sense. Occasionally, to our dismay, a plant received an unnecessary pruning, but his browsing was not extensive; a mouthful here and there satisfied, without devastation of any one plant or shrub, and it was not difficult to keep him off by putting up a few peasticks around the most valued plants.

I hoped that by offering food I might divert him from temptation, but he ignored every item on the menu. In this I was at first influenced by a keeper at the London zoo who told me that his captive muntjac usually took dairy nuts, or brown bread if these were not available. From later experience I realise that his deer must have been very hungry to accept this unaccustomed diet, and I wish I had then had more knowledge of muntjac's feeding habits in the wild, and could have offered some helpful suggestions.

In winter 1961 I began watching again in the garden, and spent long, cold vigils in moonlight which sometimes brought reward, and on dark nights I had success on occasions using a torch. But there was always a risk of disturbance: one false step on a twig, one unexpected meeting on the way back to the house, might jeopardise the chance of the deer's remaining in the garden.

In the early spring of the following year the buck gave us some delightful watching when he came near the house in daylight, and strolled casually through the garden. I also continued my watching by night, when sometimes he lay ruminating under the pines, and I was able to use a torch without disturbing him. He looked towards the light, but seemed not to connect it with human presence, as he continued to chew contentedly, sometimes shutting his eyes for a while, half asleep. One night, finding the cold too intense to be endured for long, I crept back to the house, and having warmed myself by the fire, returned later. He was still where I had left him, chewing, relaxed and apparently happy in the belief that at this hour the garden was his, and his alone.

During the spring and summer of 1962 I added little to my knowledge of the ways of muntjac but I saw the deer from time to time, and slots and other signs showed that they were still using the territory, though unlike the visiting crossbills, who swept down to the birds' pools in a whirl of light, colour, and ringing calls, they took their pleasures silently.

# CHAPTER 2

# More than Shadows

THE winter of 1962–63 began early. On the first bitter winds countless birds flocked to the garden in search of food. Many were strangers, as the greenfinches, hundreds strong, which swept into the birches, rising to hang in a twittering cloud on the wind before drifting away, their fate unknown. Later, with many more, came redwings and fieldfares searching the berried shrubs; scrambling for rotting crabs on the bough. It was difficult to count the innumerable tits that came to my hand; with them the long-tails of previous winters, though this time generous supplies of food could not save all.

The first snow came on 11 December and fell intermittently till dawn, clear and brilliant with moonlight touching the birches, white against a frosty sky.

I wondered how the deer would withstand a severe winter. Muntjac have been known to die in numbers from exposure and lack of food when all was snow covered. But if the deer in the garden would take food put out for them, and accept man-made shelter, they at least might be helped. A further cold spell began over Christmas, and I set to work in one of the thickets to build a span shelter from stakes reinforced with pea-sticks, which I thatched with a thick layer of bracken, making it more or less wind and weather proof. A dry bed of hay added to indoor comfort. Next morning there was a fresh fall of snow, and in a few days, slots leading in and out showed that the shelter had been discovered and was already in use.

The beauty of that winter will always be remembered though the suffering it brought to wild life and indeed to all who were exposed to its arctic conditions tempered most people's appreciation. But snow brings a breadth and simplicity to the landscape which does much to obliterate the scars of modern development. For me it has an irresistible lure, and I am usually out early on my way to the nearest badgers' sett. It is a rare experience to be in the field before human footfall has shattered the wide expanse—

the silence, the clear air, the sense of remoteness are compelling.
This morning I was set on reaching a wood that I knew to be
shared by foxes, badgers and muntjac. After an earlier light fall of
snow I found that Brock had been very active through the night;
foxes too had ranged widely, and the neat slots of muntjac were
looped across the open woodland where hummocks of bracken
were snow covered, forming igloos, possibly appreciated by deer.
On this later visit I found drifting snow across the entrances to the
badgers' sett, and no spoor visible. There were no tracks of deer or
fox, and from the complete stillness one might suppose the wood
devoid of life. Doubtless the badgers were secure in their sett, the
fox probably also underground, and the deer watching from some
snow-covered lair under the brambles. I stayed for a while to make
sketches of the snowbound sett, though the cold was so intense that
I could scarcely hold a pencil. It seemed impossible that any life
unused to such conditions could survive, particularly if no food
were found. Carnivores, as fox and badger, might subsist on dead
birds and other victims of the cold, but there was little hope for
hungry deer. Further blizzards were on the way, and the next

9

time I tried to reach the wood I was forced to return, having fallen into snowdrifts almost shoulder high.

At home it was difficult to provide enough food for the hungry flocks that descended on the sanctuary. Everything edible was readily devoured by the birds, though strangely the deer still despised my offerings, and were presumably living on a meagre fare of ivy and young shoots of holly. One day I found that the buck had been routing for conkers under the trees along the boundary, though most had been taken by grey squirrels in the previous autumn. Thinking he might return, I put down some apples and brown bread. These disappeared overnight, and I thought he had taken some as his slots were in the surrounding snow. Unfortunately when I was renewing the supply in the afternoon, we met! He was away at once in long leaps, and I did not find his tracks there again. But I put some food beside one of the paths he was using, and it was all gone by morning. Slots again showed that he had come to it, but many animals were hungry in the cold and tracks suggested that others had taken a share.

The buck was now seen not infrequently by day as he had become more tolerant in the cold weather. He often lay for a long time under a holly hedge not far from the house, or in any similar place that offered shelter. Securely hidden he was sometimes not seen till too late, and broke cover. As trespassers in our own garden we crept about, peering furtively into thickets as we passed, anxious not to disturb him if it could be avoided, though he rarely showed·panic, and took to his feet reluctantly, to walk away and stand watching the intruders before wandering again into cover. He appeared to have settled down in the garden, and often remained within a small area all day. By using binoculars I was able to get detailed views, and I saw that his ears were now badly torn. Muntjac seem prone to ear damage, received perhaps in conflict with other bucks, though some are scarred deliberately by marking, when a right-angled notch is cut from the ear to enable observers to record the animal's numbers and whereabouts. The preliminary chase by dogs into a net creates terror and risk to the deer, especially to muntjac does, which may be in fawn at any time, but those who use such methods have few scruples. In the Highlands many red deer calves are marked soon after birth by tags in both ears. This is more humane as they are easily caught at an early age, though the result is still unsightly. A further method, which is much criticised by thinking naturalists, is the insertion of a radio under the skin as a means of tracing the animal's movements. It is hoped that the coloured collars containing radios, now being used on deer, will replace this, though I find myself in agreement with the comment (made surprisingly by a burly policeman) that a marked animal is in some way unclean, has lost its charm.

If marking is not strictly limited and some restraint put upon the over zealous, a time may come when we shall see few wild animals that are not disfigured; when all will be tabulated and filed; the aesthetics of nature no longer valued.

From the beginning of my observations on deer in the garden I decided against any attempt to mark them. Apart from humane considerations, I felt that the advantages would not outweigh those of getting to know and recognise the deer as individuals, which could be achieved only by retaining the garden as a place where they would feel secure from such disturbance.

# Muntjac

The question of what we should or should not do to animals to increase our knowledge goes much further than marking. The ethics of the subject are deeply involved. Upon wild animals, for which there is little or no protection, experiments by a section of too ardent biologists have much increased over the past few years, and the argument that this benefits the species of the animal involved is put forward but rarely justified. Many experiments are purely a means of satisfying man's curiosity, and those who conduct them would do well to search their consciences. At a time when science has pride of place and brings prestige to those who practise it, the temptation to ignore the welfare of animals is all too great. The science of the field naturalist, who puts consideration for the animals first, often brings more revelations than the work of the scientist in his laboratory. Much valuable knowledge can be gained by exerting patience and watching animals in the field where natural behaviour is a reliable asset. There are of course some facts which cannot be known without biological research, but it is neither desirable nor necessary for wild life to be subjected to terror and pain in the laboratory to satisfy our desire for learning. Requests and advertisements asking for wild animals, dead or alive, for experiment, besides their sinister implications, are a drain on our diminishing fauna. Dissection can give many answers, but animals should not be killed especially for the purpose. Sufficient are found dead on the roads; still more are destroyed by farmers and keepers, and these together with the deer culled annually by foresters are enough to satisfy the needs of the most avid biologists. All this causes enough suffering, and loss of our native wild life without adding to the toll. The increase of deer in some districts presents a problem, but muntjac, foresters tell me, do no harm to their interest. Yet they are culled regardless of the fact that there is no season in which this can be done without young fawns, still dependent on the does, being left to die from starvation, as births can occur in any month.

Threats of this always hung over the garden deer, as I assumed they wandered some distance over the countryside, and I occasionally had reports of a cull having taken place.

Towards the end of February 1963 I found smaller slots beside those of the buck, and concluded he had the company of a doe, perhaps the original one. There were signs of much wandering by both, though I usually saw only the buck.

## More than Shadows

Deer and snow are complimentary, each a foil to the other's beauty. Watching the deer, whether at gaze or leaping over the unbroken snow was a measure of recompense for the prolonged bitterness of winter. And now, at last I was able to feed them regularly, as they were coming each night for food put out in a wild part of the garden, where they were sometimes joined by a hare who had taken refuge in the undergrowth, having come in from open fields. In a short time, tracks running in circles, figures of eight, and forms in the snow, indicated that more than one hare was involved in nightly revels.

Any food scattered by bird lovers was a godsend to wild life, though probably few people realised that it was also needed by animals at night. Foxes, badgers and other mainly nocturnal mammals were desperate with hunger, and would eat almost anything. Every naturalist remembers the sad record of that winter. Thousands of birds perished; many deer, and doubtless the weaker among other species, succumbed to cold and hunger. Possibly the small mammals found food and shelter more easily. Short-tailed voles were said to have lived well under snow-covered

grass, where they were able to breed successfully in some districts. It was difficult to assess losses in the garden. Water shrews seemed to have disappeared when spring came, and field-mice and bank-voles were probably much reduced; for the first time in many years *Heleborous orientalis*, and species of scilla and crocus flowered with abandon though usually much of the bloom is taken by voles and field-mice.

The severe weather brought a marked degree of tameness in birds and in some mammals. The buck of the garden was more confiding, and on an estate where I had further facilities to study muntjac, both buck and doe, resident there, were coming out into the open to feed by day on apples put down for them by the head gardener. The buck was exceptionally tolerant, and continued to feed in view of the gardeners at work, or myself sketching. But when the thaw came, the deer retired to another part of the estate, and watching there was once more a game of chance.

I wondered if the deer of our garden would change their terri-tory, but they remained, and were still frequenting it when the chiffchaff heralded the arrival of spring on 4 April.

Soon muntjac activity was almost veiled by foliage, and there seemed little hope of encountering the deer, though I sometimes heard them barking in the early morning. I had recently sent to a gunsmith in London for a roe-call, a device used by stalkers to bring unfortunate bucks within range of the rifle. I had in mind that muntjac might also be called up in this way and brought within sketching distance. The recent barking suggested a rutting season, said to be the best time to attempt to call roe. I had little faith in the experiment, but at sundown hid myself in the brush-wood round the base of an elm overlooking the wood, which was often frequented by the deer. Though I had no clear conception of a call which would attract muntjac, I blew hopefully on the whistle, at the same time manipulating the flow of air with my fingers. The sound that came forth was unlike any I had heard, or have since heard made by muntjac, but, to my surprise, almost at once the buck answered. I replied on the whistle, and he barked again. I heard the patter of his hoofs as he came towards me, and I repeated the call. He moved nearer, and I could then see him as he stood below the bank where I was hidden; his head up, ears forward listening intently. But he was too close for further experi-ment, which would almost certainly have given me away. Presently he wandered off, and after a few minutes I called again. To each call he replied, but eventually his barking became so insistent that I thought he had probably discovered the ruse and was frightened. This did not fit in with my plans to encourage the deer to stay in the garden, and I put off further attempts for the time being.

# CHAPTER 3

# Into the Light

THE mystery surrounding the lives of wild creatures makes the naturalist's task difficult. In few mammals is this more apparent than in the small Asiatic deer. So far their story lacked detail and continuity. I began to wonder if I would progress any further with a species so secretive and difficult to observe. But the buck, at least, was gradually becoming less retiring. If he was lying-up in cover we could often continue gardening a short distance away without disturbance, unless we inadvertently went very close to his retreat. He was bolder than the doe, and consequently more often encountered, but he planned his movements to keep a limited distance between himself and mankind. He seemed to know, either by instinct or deduction, that the gardener could not wheel his barrow between the currant bushes where he had his lair. He allowed him to pass and to empty his barrow a short distance away, and while this routine continued the deer remained, watching. But if the gardener stopped on the path to adjust his load, suspicion was immediately aroused, and the deer was up and away, disclosing his whereabouts, which would otherwise have passed unnoticed. His intuition led him so far but not far enough to enable him to discriminate between innocent and threatening human behaviour.

We often saw the buck in the garden throughout the year, though slots were the only indication that the doe was still in the territory. But early in December I found the tracks of a very small fawn beside those of the doe, and in the second week of January 1964 came across them again.

I had made some new bracken shelters during the past year, and tracks leading in and out showed that they were in use. I had tempted the deer by leaving food in the shelters, but this seemed not to be the only attraction as in some I found deer-shaped hollows in the bedding where they had been lying. I had collected sweet chestnuts and conkers from the woods during the previous autumn, and these with apples were taken readily. If any apples were left they were always Bramleys; Coxes it seemed were pre-

ferred for their sweetness. The buck also took food put out in the
water garden at a short distance from the summerhouse, which
formed a secure hide for the watcher. I could sit there and wait in
comparative comfort, my binoculars at the ready. With a good pair
of night glasses one can see much that is normally hidden from the
naked eye, and I was able to watch the buck feeding in the dusk or
in moonlight, his ears flicking to catch the least alien sound but
unaware that he was being watched. These views were obtained
in some discomfort as the nights were bitterly cold, and it was
necessary to reach the summerhouse well before the deer was likely
to be in the area. The whole manoeuvre was risky, as there was
always a chance of coming upon him unexpectedly. One night I
arrived when he was already by the food. He leapt away expressing
his annoyance in a series of short barks growing fainter as he
retreated, and I knew I had lost his company at least for that night.
He disliked being caught out in the open, but unlike muntjac I
had previously encountered in the wild, who sometimes stood
barking defiance for as long as half-an-hour, he usually seemed
anxious only to retreat a short distance, then stand at gaze taking
stock of my credentials before drifting away. This I concluded was
as near to friendship as I was ever likely to get.

Mammals who retire to den or burrow are comparatively easy
to observe. If an occupied earth or sett is located one has a fair
chance of seeing the animals emerge. The badger usually comes
above ground at regular times in the evening, and once these are

known some good watching is assured. It is possible also to follow badgers after they leave the sett, if one has acquired cat's feet and a full measure of stealth. I have often watched them feeding on open fields, or bringing in their bedding—a fascinating ritual— or crept up to their setts in the early hours to wait for their return at dawn, passing them sometimes on the way as they routed noisily under the hedgerows. This is not a difficult manoeuvre if one is careful to keep down wind, for at that hour they are not expecting human company.

Though it was enjoyable to see the buck by night, apart from moonlight, visibility was often poor, and I would have preferred to watch him feeding in daylight. Food disappeared during the day, and I found fresh slots where it had been put down. It was easy to see, by the manner of feeding, whether deer or others had taken it. Deer left the shucks of chestnuts and conkers, chewed, on the ground, but squirrels carried each away intact to be nibbled while held in the paws. And one could of course see the varying sizes of teeth marks, and the marks of birds' beaks on apples.

So far the deer had rarely come near the house, and I thought he was unlikely to feed there, but one morning his slots were on the lawn not far from the windows, and I found he had been tasting some of the apples left by the birds. I quickly took advantage of this and put food there every evening. The weather was very cold with twelve to sixteen degrees of frost overnight, and there were signs that he came there during the dark hours to feed. One evening I put some apples still nearer the house, tempting him with Coxes. He took them, and from his slots I saw that he had ventured to the edge of the steps below the pergola.

Every night the apples disappeared, but not before the house was in darkness. I spent most of my evenings watching till late from the window of a dark and very cold room overlooking the feeding ground, but sometimes the cold damped my enthusiasm, and I crept back to the fireside in the sitting room. One night I was tempted to stay too long, and when I returned I found that some of the apple had been taken meanwhile. Next evening I waited more patiently but still failed to see him. In the morning not a scrap of apple remained!

Most wild life observation is at times frustrating, but no species could more cunningly devise means to outwit the inquisitive

watcher. Fresh slots about the garden showed that the buck still wandered there by day, quietly moving from cover to cover, always seeing before being seen; watching every move on my part, and allowing only a limited approach.

The garden could not be overlooked as a wide open space from the windows. It was not designed to be seen in entirety at a glance. There were many hidden paths, secret ways and thickets, all of which made it especially attractive to the deer but increased the watcher's difficulties. It was hard to resist the temptation to go out and look for him, and one afternoon finding new slots a stone's throw from the house, I dispensed with caution and followed. They led to the top of a bank above the tennis court. There, suddenly, perhaps because he had sensed my approach, he had leapt away over the snow, clearing the open space in long leaps—nine—eight—seven feet apart! the distance lessening as he slowed to a run. In the wood he had tripped lightly to the cover of some hazel bushes, then wandered up the slope under the wych elms, where I saw him now, poised against the white expanse.

Instinct which prompts an animal to live under cover is unevenly shared in the wild: some are endowed with the comfort of an underground burrow, others, as deer or hare, must exist more or less in the open through all weather. Here in the garden the deer were fortunate; they were never short of food, and compared to those in outlying woods, they lived well.

This fine view of the buck renewed my enthusiasm for further outdoor watching but the weather was exceptionally cold with snow lying and heavy frosts overnight, and this drove me once more to revert to the window. One evening to my joy I saw the buck arrive early. He crept up the grass walk, and keeping his body in the shadows, stretched forward to snatch a piece of apple from within the light. He was soon tempted again in spite of his early hesitation and next evening was even more confident. After a few visits he came fully into the light, and I was able to make some quick sketches. This was not easy in a dark room, but I held a small torch to the paper, hoping the light would not show me to the deer outside.

At that time the buck was, I thought, going to the woods by day, as his tracks were often on the banks of the lane. On the way he crossed the opposite garden where outside lights were often kept on during the evening on house and garage walls. Unfortunately they were sometimes not turned out till late or all night, and when this happened the deer did not come. It seemed that while he would tolerate some light if the lure of food was strong, he would not cross a well lit area if he could avoid it.

I felt that the more tempting I could make the menu the more frequently and earlier he would come. When I had first attempted to feed the deer I had put out whole apples. These were persistently ignored, and it was not till I cut them into quarters, that he became interested. This could have been chance, though pieces were, of course, easier to bite, and the stronger scent from cut apples may have attracted him. We had harvested a good crop of Coxes from our orchard in the past autumn, and these were taken with apparent relish, but they began to diminish, and I then put out some Bramleys. He left these, yet took any Coxes that were with them. He had shown his preference for sweet apples before, and I could foresee a time in the near future when I would lose him if I had only sour cookers to offer. Next evening I sprinkled sugar over some of the cut Bramleys, leaving a separate pile unsweetened. In the morning, all but the unsweetened apples had been taken. He was very selective in his choice taking first Coxes, then pears, if there were any, then sweetened Bramleys. He sniffed the hedgehog's cheese more with suspicion than interest, disdaining even the best

pink Cheshire. It was always interesting to put out an addition to
the menu, and watch his reactions; the cautious sniffing of any food
that was strange to him; the complete disregard of some which I
thought would be acceptable. All food, with few exceptions, was
usually cleared overnight, and doubtless field-mice and hedgehogs accounted for a share. It disappeared also in wild parts of the
garden, and there, from tracks near-by, I though the doe too was
feeding.

Sweet chestnuts had always been a favourite, but as with Coxes,
the supply was running out. Though I toured the local shops the
season was over, and I could get only a few that were past their
prime. Conkers also were scarce, and once more I was faced with
the problem of how to retain the deer's company. I noticed that
rose hips were taken in the garden. In one place the buck's slots
showed where he had stretched up, seemingly in an upright posture
on his hind legs, to reach those far above his normal browsing level.
But when I plucked some hips, and put them out with other food,

they were not eaten. Apparently, being out of context, as it were, their succulent qualities were not recognised.

One night the hedgehog's visit coincided with the deer's feeding time. It ignored the approach of the buck, having started to feed from its dish, and the buck in turn seemed not to notice the hedgehog till he lowered his head to the apples. He stared in astonishment, indignant perhaps that this diminutive creature had the audacity to invade his feeding territory. He took some apple, and began to eat, but suddenly, without warning, leapt off the ground to come down almost astride the feeding hedgehog! The shock galvanised it into action! It scuttled away, tumbling over itself with anxiety, and was not seen again that night.

By mid-March the buck was still coming to feed by the house, and a late fall of snow increased his appetite. He was using the bracken shelters again, though for a while he had deserted them, and had been lying-up frequently among ivy under the pines. This area had probably been used by the buck and doe for some time. Ivy was plucked over a wide expanse, and bare hollows worn in the herbage where they lay ruminating. The deer had always liked this part of the garden where ivy was thick under pines which topped a grassy slope. Small bushes there gave cover, for the area was left wild. The deer also had a good view over surrounding land, but they seemed unaware of my hide in the hedge about thirty yards away, from where I sometimes watched them by moonlight.

The doe was very shy, but the buck was gradually becoming bolder. I saw him watching occasionally from beyond the bushes when I came out with food. I tried to avoid clashing with his arrival but timing was difficult in the evening: if the food was there too early, birds and squirrels raided it; if too late, the buck might come to find the feeding ground empty. His disappointment was obvious. Sometimes a few conkers remained in spite of the ravages of squirrels, but this was a poor substitute for the usual meal, and he continued to rout for a long time under the heap of hay where, in an effort to outwit the squirrels, I usually hid some of the food. But they soon discovered it, and when they had been there first, he seemed unable to believe that even this source had failed. He searched long and disconsolately, then wandered away. I had then to creep out with more food, hoping he would return later.

## Into the Light

His demands had lessened since April, for there was plenty of fresh leafage everywhere, and it was surprising that he came to feed at all. His visits reduced as May advanced, and he stopped coming throughout the summer. But he was still about the garden, and in July several nights of intermittent barking suggested the possibility of a rutting season.

Muntjac fawns may be born at any time of year in Britain, but the period between the rut and the birth of the fawn was not known. From later observation I learned that mating appears to follow closely upon the birth of the young, and at rutting or thereabouts one may hope to see a new fawn. But it was not till October that I found the slots of this one, and by chance a few days later saw it in the water garden. It appeared to be of the right age: two to three months, and strolled by a short distance away, wandering idly into cover without noticing the watchers.

Summer fawns can hide almost completely in thick herbage, their existence unknown even to the searching naturalist. Apart from the tell-tale slots, this one might have kept its secret till now. The wild parts of the garden, which were the deer's favourite haunts, had many tangled areas the depths of which were known only to them and to the nesting birds, specially to blackcaps, lovers of wild rose and bramble thickets. Three or four pairs nest yearly in the sanctuary; one in the water garden, where their chief nesting site is a thick bush of *Rosa arvensis;* another in the bamboos, and a third in a bramble thicket in view of the studio windows. From there one spring I watched a cock building a nest

23

foundation to lure his mate to the hawthorn bush of his choice a few yards from the window. His song had been ecstatic for the past week, and now, alighting on the tamarisk he plucked vigorously at some small dead twigs, till at last detaching one, he opened his beak in a fresh burst of song, and it fell to the ground. This happened repeatedly, with the bird using his pent up energy gathering nesting material which was each time lost in renewed song.

The platform, this mere hint of a nest, is so frail that it is often difficult to find, but I have seen as many as five constructed in a very small area of territory, presumably by the same bird. The cock blackcap takes an active part in rearing the young, sharing with the hen the incubation of the eggs and brooding the nestlings. During this time his song diminishes, but regains its full vigour with the onset of a second brood, which is not unusual.

I would find it hard to live where the blackcap's song is not part of the music of spring and early summer. It is exceptionally loud and rich in timbre for a small bird, and the clear fluting notes are delivered with a brilliance of technique which leaves the bird with few rivals among the warblers. Some blackcaps are of course better songsters than others, and have a wider vocabulary. It is possible to identify individuals by voice where several are present in a district. One of our spinney is known by the song-thrush notes included in his repertoire; an accomplishment regarded as mimicry.

Early in July it is all over. Though adults and young may be seen bathing in the garden pools, the blackcaps are almost silent. Their visits to the fruiting elder bushes in October may be the last we shall see of them before next spring. It was in the hope of watching departing warblers that we had come to the water garden on the day the fawn was encountered. But she too was to disappear for a while, though I found her slots beside those of the doe, and alone as she grew more independent. She usually remained in hiding, and it was not till December that I saw the doe and fawn together, browsing under the pines. They were off at once, tails up, their targets snow-white against the dark winter terrain.

During the week of Christmas 1964 a new buck was seen in the orchard. From that time the one with the tattered ears vanished, and his going was a mystery. The stranger was younger; very dapper, with short antlers, and ears unscarred.

# CHAPTER 4

# An April Fawn

THE new year started well. One frosty morning, brilliant with sunshine, I looked out from the studio window to see the buck and doe, with the pheasants, sunning themselves under the big oak. They strolled down the grass slope opposite the window, completely at ease, the colour and gloss of their coats heightened by the sunlight and clear frosty air. They were in no hurry and stayed for nearly half-an-hour, giving me a chance to make notes of their winter pelage and any individual features for future recognition. There was a marked difference in their colour; for the doe in winter is dark chocolate brown on the back, and the buck a rich chestnut. Otherwise the general colour of both was reddish gold. The buck had no white except under the tail, but the doe was cleanly marked with white on chin, neck, chest, and belly. The legs of both appeared dusky, but light on the inner side.

They wandered idly, pausing here and there to browse from the ivy or grass at their feet; tastefully plucking a flower head of *Petasites fragrans* in passing, and once to my dismay, a mouthful of iris. If the deer took a liking to these the result could be disastrous. For my sister, the raising of new hybrids is a major interest. Fortunately they were, it seemed, unpalatable, as no more were taken. The possibility that the deer's fancy might turn to irises was one I dared not contemplate. A single night's activity among the seedlings would eliminate the results of years of hybridising.

Though the deer had appeared miraculously under the studio window, they were not coming, as the buck of previous years, to feed near the house, and I soon reverted to watching again out-of-doors, hoping to attract them with food near their accustomed paths. I took up my stand in an almost ready-made hide in an old ash stub overlooking one of their runways a short distance away; it was also a feeding place where they often stopped to browse from ivy on the hedge. But I was at that time unlucky with the weather. Though the moon was up and giving a good light, the nights were bitterly cold with high winds, and shadows in continual motion.

25

The light and movement combined did not produce conditions in which deer, timid at all times, were likely to come into the open, and I had no success. But snowfall which soon followed revealed the buck's slots near the house. Perhaps I should have limited the food to a position by the windows only, but such weather called for generosity, and I distributed it in a number of places in the garden. None was overlooked, and within a week the new buck was coming into the light from the window to feed. I also saw the fawn occasionally among the shadows.

How far the deer wandered from the garden I could not tell. Roe deer, *Capreolus capreolus*, are known to range several miles from home ground at times, and the movements of muntjac in this respect are probably similar. The deer in the garden had always been used to coming and going freely through hedges on every side, and they had several paths through the broken down fence on the south boundary. But a new neighbour, wishing to keep his labrador under control, erected a five-foot fence of chestnut paling there, and the deer could no longer go out in that direction. But after a time I saw that they had been squeezing through the widest gaps between the pales, and one day the fence nearly brought disaster. When taking food to a shelter, I put up the doe from some bushes near the boundary. Caught unaware, instead of taking the easy course of running left or right she rushed at the fence and leapt through a five-inch gap below the top straining wire. In this way she might have gone through, but as she came down, the gap narrowed at the centre wire, and she was held at the waist. At once in desperate panic she began to bark hysterically; unable to reach the ground on either side and kicking out violently with her back legs. As I came to her aid, the barking rose to continuous ear-splitting screams, and I remember wondering if the next-door dog was at home and would come racing to attack. Something had to be done quickly. I grasped the deer's legs, and tried to lift her, but she was stuck fast. In the renewed terror my attempts created, her struggles became so violent that she seemed likely to injure herself. Possible solutions raced through my mind, but time was short, and I decided to try again. At first my efforts seemed to have no effect, then suddenly, she was free—away through the bushes so fast that it was impossible to know whether she was physically injured, though she left a mass of fur adhered to the palings, and was not seen again for nearly two weeks.

But the buck continued to come nightly for food, and dined sometimes with the pheasants soon after dawn. I saw him almost every evening till the second week in April.

It is difficult to name the most beautiful month of spring, but April has many claims when the leaves are unfolding, not yet casting their full shade, when shadows are still delicate in form, crisp on the bare fields and over tree trunks green with lichen, brilliant in the new sunlight; when each fresh sign of spring is an escape from winter; the first flowers, the song, the nest, the earliest fledgelings—all are soon gone, with spring pressing on through May to the wild rose and summer.

It was mid-April when we discovered the spotted fawn; appearing as it were from nowhere—and soon nowhere found, for it needed little herbage to conceal his tiny form, and he was easily missed as he lay in dappled shadow, though sometimes we came upon him, seemingly unafraid, gazing out, silent and illusory from his sanctuary beyond the foliage or honeysuckle bines.

These early weeks in the fawn's life were favoured by clear days when I felt reluctant to leave the garden breaking into leaf and flower; the birds nesting; the fawn always offering the possibility of encounter. Yet at this time of year I am drawn to the open countryside, alive with activity, where at night the lapwing calls, wheeling and tumbling about the moonlit sky, and fox and badger cubs are coming above ground—when all life is stirring and the young, radiant in the few short brilliant weeks in which they grow from first emergence to the sobriety of later days—for naturalists a season of discovery; much to see, and time always too short.

Watching by night is irresistible, but too much, even by those of good intention, can cause interference; a contingency which may, with the increasing popularity of wild life study among large communities, eventually make life difficult for the animals to the point of limiting their breeding activity. Badger watching, once the interest of a few enlightened naturalists, has become fashionable, and may contribute to the decline in the badger's breeding, which is now occurring, and is thought to be largely due to the animals becoming sterile through toxic poisons on the land. Wild life observation is at its best a solitary occupation and should be confined to small numbers—not more than two or three people at at time. Watchers *en masse* see little and may do considerable harm if their activities are persistent.

But the chief danger to the badger is still the frequent gassing which takes place widely in the countryside in spite of the fact that this and poisoning, which also occurrs, are illegal. Over the past ten years or so the destruction has increased and I know of many thriving colonies, in my district alone, which have been extinguished in this way. Some farmers destroy badgers, but they are more often the victims of gamekeepers working for shooting syndicates. Their activities sometimes extend far beyond the boundaries of the land on which they are employed, and one cannot hope to find any setts unmolested over a considerable area

## An April Fawn

surrounding such estates. Farmers are all too ready to allow the gassing of badgers on their land should a keeper ask permission to destroy them. His usual pretext is that the badger is an habitual killer of game and poultry. This is entirely erroneous. Proved instances are so rare as to be unworthy of mention. In fact the badger, who is through ignorance, often blamed for the misdeeds of the fox, is listed by the Ministry of Agriculture as beneficial to the land, with the advice that he should not be molested. His diet includes many small rodents, young rabbits and harmful grubs and those who have a badgers sett on their land should be thankful. If the persecution, which has always been heavy, continues at the present rate, Hertfordshire at least is likely to lose the badger as a member of its fauna.

Why, I am sometimes asked, is this allowed to go on? In most cases proof of the identity of the killer is hard to obtain. Badgers' setts are mostly in unfrequented areas, and farm-workers, who are likely witnesses, are almost never prepared to give evidence in the court against a local man. But there have been prosecutions, and anyone finding a sett gassed should report it at once to their County Trust or to The Fauna Preservation Society at Regent's Park.

Animals whose way of life accommodates them underground are vulnerable to this devastating form of attack, from which, fortunately, deer are exempt, though they are more often the target of the man or boy with a shot-gun, and the cruelty of the deer snare is well known. For some species too there is the menace of the hunt. It is not surprising that the wild animals of our countryside are shy and rarely encountered without much patience and stealth.

Difficulty in watching deer occurs through their keen sensitivity and protective instinct to keep on the move. Though muntjac may be located in a sanctuary by day, and expected to emerge at sundown, they sometimes wander afield before evening, and one can easily be thwarted by their going out unseen on the other side of the thicket, leaving the watcher waiting indefinitely while they wander perhaps acres distant. A hide in a tree is helpful, and some practical examples are illustrated in the *Field Guide to British Deer* published by the Mammal Society.

This spring the fawn's presence brought a special interest to the garden. Its arrival outshone most other events of the season: the finding of fox cubs in a hidden dell (where I watched them playing

29

in the evening light, and which grew to maturity, as no one else discovered the earth well screened by a steep bank of nettles) the badger cubs emerging early from my favourite sett; roding wood-cock flying against a pale moon; nightingales, and the reeling of grasshopper warblers; nightjars too, in the old adjacent wood.

Because the fawn had encountered us in the garden from the beginning of life he was not exceptionally timid. He stared back when discovered, wondering perhaps whether he should abandon the security of his hiding place for the doubtful safety of the open where, in spite of his natural speed, he would be exposed to the unknown. Though seemingly at ease, one felt that he was taut as a drawn bow, and would vanish at the least whisper of alarm. When I came across him I froze at once, and as we stared at one another I scarcely dared to breathe least he took flight. But on occasions when he did decide to leave, he slipped quietly away, and his going had been so illusory that I was left with a feeling of unreality.

In such encounters one comes very near to nature, and the desire for some form of communication which will arrest the attention and bring the animal even closer, is great. A fox cub can be called by a shrill squeak from pursed lips, and will come to investigate. As a carnivore his living depends on hunting, and the squeak of a mouse, or a squealing rabbit brings him at once to the quarry. But for the deer, vegetarian by nature, these have no appeal. One day when I found the fawn lying under a hedge, I tried the experiment, with disappointing results. He was immediately alerted; tensed, he got to his feet and with a look of disdain, tripped lightly out of view.

Probably the deer's only response to the cry of another animal is fear, as he senses from it a warning of danger. For his protection he relies almost entirely on speed, and is likely at once to be up and away! But an adult muntjac may if cornered put up a good fight, tearing its aggressor with the hoofs, and the buck by using the additional weapon of the small tusks, carried in the upper jaw. But deer are poorly equipped for defence in comparison with the carnivores, and consequently anxious to avoid conflict. Their extreme timidity keeps them alert to danger, and no one is ever likely to tame a muntjac. They do not take kindly to captivity, and it was noticeable that the buck I saw in the London zoo allowed his keeper no liberties, and always kept him at a distance.

Much useful sketching can be done in zoos though I prefer if possible to draw animals in the wild. Caged, they make sad company, and I find the atmosphere of a zoo uninspiring. The animals have lost their natural freshness and vitality of spirit. Even the young compare sadly with their wild counterparts. There is a unique charm in the fawn or fox cub in its natural environment; in the otter coursing the stream—in any animal that is truly wild. The free life, though often short, seems a more desirable state than security long confined.

The catching of wild animals for zoos is a distressing process, and how much the animal suffers from loss of its normal habitat and way of life cannot be assessed. To those born in captivity confinement is doubtless more easily endured. But even in the best of zoos one sometimes sees animals in unsuitable quarters, with the larger mammals pacing to and fro in small enclosures, though much is now being done to alleviate this by rebuilding in the long established zoos.

Too many animal parks and zoos are being set up with a view to financial reward, and some with little consideration for the animals contained. These additions keep up the demand for the capture of wild animals, and the numbers should be severely limited. Admittedly when a species is becoming extinct or its habitat destroyed it may be saved by preservation of some of its members in captivity, but a certain standard of accommodation should be enforced in every zoo. It would be helpful too if facilities were provided in each case for the animals to indulge their instinctive habits, as the badgers' urge to dig (which they cannot do confined in a concrete enclosure) the desperate need of the otter to swim and dive; of the monkey or squirrel to climb. It should not be difficult to supply a concrete soil-filled pit, in which burrowing animals cannot escape, yet may satisfy their instinct to excavate. Water is vital for those who need to swim, and trees for animals of climbing habit. These and other such amenities for the variety of species concerned are necessary for the animals' contentment, and their indulgence in normal activites has an educational value for the visitor to the zoo.

But it is to the wild that we turn for entirely natural behaviour, and this can be seen at its best in the hours of twilight, when the fear of encounter with man is small and the animals relaxed. Then, if one can remain concealed, the effort and discomfort entailed is forgotten in the pleasure of watching. The field naturalist endures much from the weather, and if this is fair midges are abroad and hungry, but they are preferable to the icy wind, which finds its way through even the warmest clothing. It would be convenient if a number of tractors could be left out on the fields in strategic positions for the use of naturalists. It is not often that one is blessed with this rare luxury, but when the afternoon turned too wet for Will to continue the rolling, he was forced to leave the tractor marooned on the field till the ground should be dry enough to move it without damage to the crop. I had the use of the cab meanwhile, a boon in all weather, and an excellent hide, though draughty, as the glass had long since gone from the rear windows. Wildlife is normally unafraid of machines on the land, and seems rarely to connect them with mankind.

Before leaving the tractor, Will had noticed flattened herbage on the edge of a small undisturbed area of grass and nettles that topped the banks of a ditch and the entrance to a field drain. Badgers had stayed here for a while in summer, taking bedding into the culvert, and a vixen was possibly now sheltering her cubs there. The earth was reasonably safe from interference as the land was not often frequented; it was some way from any farm track and consisted mostly of growing crops. The ditch was now almost dry, but heavy storm water would quickly make the culvert a death-trap for cubs.

The fortunate position of the tractor gave a view over a wide area of land, and the field drain was only a short distance away. But the foxes' earth had one feature overwhelmingly in the animals' favour; the entrance lay entirely hidden between the steep banks of the ditch. Herbage above added at least another two feet to the screen. But my hopes were pinned on the cubs' coming up to play on the area of grass they had flattened. Meanwhile I waited patiently.

Hares were browsing, their coats golden in the last rays of the sun, which had found its way between the clouds. The hares were without suspicion, as were the birds. Sedge-warblers and white-throats had recently taken up residence in the bushes along the ditch, and were calling incessantly. A cock pheasant, supposing the tractor empty, gave an unusually close view of his magnificent plumage as he strolled past in full majesty, apparently uninhibited by the fact that all his tail feathers were missing!

It was a fine evening; still, with clearing skies after the rough wind and rain in which April had passed into the first week in May.

Suddenly the fields seemed empty; even the magpie, which had been perched on top of a tall ash, disappeared. The only sign of life was on the slope of the hill below the bank that had, last year, been an area in which badgers' setts were destroyed—all holes gassed and scrub cleared in an effort to eliminate rabbits. The object of the exercise now sported happily on the field, regardless of man and fate; joy unmarred by the ability to phophesy and predict.

It was nearly nine o'clock. The birds still sang: skylarks, song-thrushes and partridges were calling. Two hares came again into view; loped and played, feeding among the new corn. The warm brown of another on the far side of the field deceived me for a moment in the false hope of the vixen's return.

Gradually the light faded and the green sweep of the corn was condensed, simplified—nothing now distracted from the breadth of the open fields, and the long undulating lines of hedges. The partridges' rhythmic rise and fall of voice was almost continuous. A pheasant on the way to his roost challenged loudly; a sharp, echoing call that shattered the still air. Then in honour to the night, the clouds, which had been lowering through most of the evening, drifted away, and the moon and the cuckoo's call came together.

I stayed on, reluctant to leave, but no foxes appeared. I was unaware that they had already vacated the earth, disturbed perhaps by the vibrations of the roller, or the rain of the past days seeping into the culvert. Though late, moonlight showed me the way back to the car, and I felt no envy for those behind the cottage windows far down the valley where the lights had gone on early.

In a few days Will reported finding the foxes' new earth on the other side of the field in an overgrown bank above a shallow ditch. I crept along the hedge to view it from a distance, and saw their playground outside, with the remnants of food that betrayed them. It was not an easy earth to watch, but I hoped to conceal myself effectively among the trees and bushes of a high bank that ran out at right angles to the one containing the earth. I found that it was already in use by the cubs. Their paths were everywhere, and I was forced to move to the bottom and stand in a bed of nettles.

Presently I looked across at the foxes' earth, and saw two little golden figures sitting on the grass outside. For some minutes they

33

An April Fawn

contemplated the diminishing sunset, then retired into the overgrown herbage below the bank. I did not see them again for nearly an hour, then suddenly, without sound, five crept out and, quickly gaining confidence, began to play; chasing one another along the edge of the field; grappling in mock battles to pounce, snap, and tumble as they rolled among the grass tussocks.

Next evening the weather was again fine, with the full moon rising long before dusk in a sky lightly touched with warm clouds. Four cubs came above ground about eight o'clock, and there was a lot of play as on the previous night. When tired of romping on the field, they all went up to the bank behind me where they were hidden from view. But I waited, and after a while they began making excursions on to the field again, where they amused themselves pouncing on imaginary mice, and shaking, the wing of a long dead rook shared as a plaything.

It is always tempting to watch the reactions of cubs to one's imitations of a mouse or squealing rabbit. Sometimes these gain only slight response; the pricking of ears, or head tilted in curiosity. But this time I was aware of a little form making its way on silent paws down the bank towards me. I squeaked again, and it came nearer, peering through the elder boughs that divided us. Within a foot or so it stopped; gazed solemnly into my face, then doubt prevailing, retreated the way it had come.

On such evenings one goes home a little lighter in spirit for the experience, however brief.

# CHAPTER 5

# Summer and Onwards

A YEAR is a long time to wait for another chance to do all one intended yet missed in the past spring. But summer too has its interests, and I usually put up my hide in the water garden where I can take stock of juvenile birds coming to drink and bathe. This year I hoped the deer might wander into the scene though I usually saw them more by chance.

Cats had caused more bird losses than usual as there had been additional building in the neighbourhood, and new families had brought their pets. Cats used to living in town delighted in the wealth of quarry the gardens and countryside provided, and they ravaged the sanctuary day and night. A tame robin, a song-thrush, a chaffinch, were among many who disappeared or were found dying. Nestlings too were taken, particularly in the early morning when cats, allowed to roam overnight, were on the spot at dawn. Numbers of birds could be saved if cat owners would keep their pets in during the night, especially over the nesting season when the young are most vulnerable. This is not difficult if the cat is habitually fed in the evening when it can be caught and shut in.

Trespassing cats are the bane of everyone who tries to give sanctuary to birds, and short of exacting the extreme penalty there is little one can do to keep them away. They seem imbued with the belief that they are sacrosanct. They fear no one, even the law is flouted, as I learned from a police constable who for years was distracted by his neighbours' cats yowling under his windows, but whose efforts to be rid of them were constantly frustrated. He saved his old police boots, and kept them ready in his bedroom where, with acquired stealth, he waited above, boot in hand, for the villains. He had plenty of practice, but though the well aimed missile sailed down, in his words, "plumb for the target every time", he never succeeded in scoring a bull's eye. Cats it seems, have a patron saint who allots to them far more than the proverbial nine lives.

Throughout the countryside they must account for a vast number of birds, and this is only one hazard. There is too the continuing toll from toxic chemicals, for which gardeners are not blameless. In spring we often lose entire broods, including warblers and tits, which we find dead in the nest through the use of poisonous sprays in surrounding gardens where the parent birds collect greenfly and caterpillars for their young. New aids tempt the gardener, and their use is advocated widely on television and radio, and in advertising campaigns. Poisonous chemicals pack the shelves of every garden supplier, and they are pressed upon a gullible public, though for most purposes the older and very effective pyrethrum (particularly in its liquid form) gives excellent results without causing harm to birds or mammals.

Though cover in July was dense, the fawn was often seen lying in some chosen place under the bushes, or wandering in daylight among the tall weeds and grass. One day I watched him sampling the first mushrooms, which had pushed up early through the dry leaves below the hedge. Muntjac are partial to fungi; I have seen them taking the small inconspicuous brown species of late summer, and a friend reported deer in her garden enjoying *Polyporus sulphureus*. But when I hoped to give them a treat by putting out mushrooms at the feeding ground, not one was eaten. They ignored too the rowan berries offered in the same way, though they made many paths under the trees, and I sometimes saw the doe and fawn there when the fruit was ripening, and berries were stripped from the lowest boughs.

In autumn I began to see more of the deer: the buck musing among the thorn bushes; the doe by the ponds; the fawn wandering alone in early mist. In October he returned to his sanctuary under the currant bushes, often lying-up there for most of the day. This seemed to be his private retreat, as I never saw other deer using it at that time. He had a slight hollow or lair in the ground to which he always returned, settling comfortably into it. How he kept warm over the long periods in which he remained there was difficult to understand, for he seemed to take little or no exercise by day. One very cold November morning when I was re-thatching one of the deer shelters, I passed his hideout several times, wheeling barrow-loads of bracken, but he watched my coming and going without concern. In the late afternoon he was still in the shelter, though he may of course have been out for a stroll meanwhile. I saw him emerge just before dusk, and make his way to the rose garden. It

would be undiplomatic to detail his menu. Generally the deer did little harm, but it was a breathless moment when a head went down to a precious plant, and one must decide between scaring the deer and watching the plant being turned into salad!

The deer had been so fastidious in their choice of apples in the past that it seemed unlikely they would eat the sour crabs now falling from the hedge, but I found they were attracted there, and one day came upon the buck and doe without warning. Though they could have put an acre between us in a few minutes, they moved off without undue hurry, and presently I saw them strolling back, making their way along the bank below the pergola. They were certainly a decorative feature of the garden; the buck was particularly handsome with antlers longer than any I had seen before on muntjac.

Soon after this the deer made a series of early morning appearances. This enabled me to do some sketching without the difficulty of holding a torch to the paper. I had begun to know the deer well, and each could be recognised. From illusive shadows of earlier years they had become a warm reality, and seemed to regard us

38

with less suspicion; a gradual advance which had been theirs, and was, I think, the result of never attempting to invade their sanctuaries, or to pursue them. The provision of food had of course been a great attraction and with the cold weather of December they began to come more often. At any time in the night I could look out of the windows and have a fair chance of seeing one or more feeding, for they came at frequent intervals.

The fawn always seemed hungry, and remained eating for long periods, which gave me plenty of sketching. It was interesting to note his gradual advance from spotted days to adolescence. He had not lost his sense of play and sometimes went off leaping across the lawn in high spirits. His coat was thick and dense; longer than in the adults, whose pelage was more sleek. It appeared velvety like the coat of a mole, and was rich in colour; a dark umber. This was relieved by a lighter, golden tone on the undersides and head, where it emphasised the typical muntjac markings. Now, at about seven-and-a-half months, he was showing distinct characteristics of a young buck, and hairy tufts defined the pedicles, beginning to grow.

Sometimes when the deer fed by day there was a mixed company, as they joined the grey squirrels, rabbits, pheasants and numerous small birds. At first the arrival of the deer caused some consternation. Blackbirds and pheasants stood back, craning their necks; apprehensive, indignant perhaps at this intrusion of what they considered to be their exclusive feeding ground. But the deer were soon accepted and even the cautious pheasants came up to feed beside them.

The relationship between deer and birds is usually one of indifference. Though I once disturbed a deer which appeared to be the cause of a robin's scolding, and on another occasion, when my protective instinct was called to the defence of a wren who was twittering anxiously in the hedge sheltering her brood, a deer moved off, though I had expected to find a cat. When the deer had gone, the scolding ceased. Perhaps the resemblance of the deer's pelage to the ginger brown of some cats awakes animosity in birds. It is unlikely that natural enmity is aroused by the gentle disposition of deer.

The fawn now seemed entirely at ease near the house, and after feeding, frequently went to a bracken shelter I had made beside one of the bamboo thickets. It was only a short distance away but he took little notice of our presence and was content to stay for long intervals showing an unusual degree of tolerance. A further surprise came one afternoon when, on my way out with food for the birds, I saw the doe with the fawn beside her, lying under the yew by the feeding ground. They were contentedly ruminating and appeared to ignore me. My sister too came out to watch, and though they were only about a dozen paces away, they made no attempt to leave, and were still there later in the afternoon.

This area under the low boughs of the yew was at that time much favoured as a place of retirement where grooming and ruminating could be indulged in at leisure. But its use in daylight soon presented a problem, as it was difficult, if not impossible to renew the supply of food with the deer almost alongside. Without food there I felt they would not continue to come, as it was their habit to ruminate for a while then go out to the feeding ground for more. Sometimes if the fawn, who was less timid than the doe, was lying under the boughs alone, I ventured out and by a devious route put apples and chestnuts down as near as possible to the usual feeding place, hoping the deer would find them. This was never entirely successful, and soon the problem became acute, with the grey squirrels even more voracious in the colder weather. They usually arrived, two or three together, and quickly disposed of all the food put out. When they could eat no more they carried the rest away, taking conkers and chestnuts one at a time to bury them at lightning speed in the flower borders. They took first the best of everything, Coxes before cooking apples; sweet chestnuts before conkers, and when all visible food was disposed of, dived down into the hay, only their tails showing as they pushed and nuzzled through it to get every scrap of food from underneath. The board was soon cleared, and repeated supplies went the same way. The grey squirrel must surely have a larger capacity for its size than any comparable species.

It was frustrating to see the deer arrive to find the cupboard bare. They sniffed disconsolately over the ground; searched under the hay, and finally wandered off. It seemed ludicrous that a few grey squirrels could upset my plans for retaining the deer by day. This was a unique opportunity for sketching and close observation, and I felt there must be some way in which food could be reserved for the deer. Selective feeding of wild life is always difficult; I had experienced it before. Squirrels can be kept from birds' food by hanging the feeders from wire that is too thin to be grasped in the paws for a descent. But the feeder must be well above ground, and certainly not near a bough or other launching place or they will take a flying leap on to it. A wire frame over the feeding table is another effective measure, but neither is of use if the competitors are deer and squirrels. Deer are shy feeders and very unlikely to take food except in natural situations: on the ground or from low growing bushes, but there was a faint hope that they might accept Coxes fixed to the bough of a shrub. I chose a branch too frail to take a squirrels weight, and cut back a few twigs making short spurs to hold the apples. But this did not deter the squirrels. They scrambled to the end, and as their weight brought the bough down, in one combined rapid movement snatched the fruit and leapt to the ground. I never succeeded in retaining an apple on the bough long enough to see whether the deer would take it. I even went to the trouble of erecting a frame from which apples could be spiked on twigs hung from thin wires. But the weakness of this was in having to dangle the food low enough to be easily reached by the deer, and the squirrels leapt up to it, hung on for a few precarious

41

moments, and again the prize was theirs. I then tried fixing apples
on top of thin, wandy sticks pushed into the ground. These flawed
them at first. They sat below, paws clasped over their already
overloaded bellies, and reviewed the situation. They soon learned
that by scrambling up a short way they could bend the sticks
over, and hanging on desperately as they see-sawed up and down,
they grabbed the apple from the top and ran off. It was amusing to
test the limit of their ingenuity; to see what they could and could
not climb. They shinned up a smooth metal pipe with ease; a thin
brass rod presented no difficulties, even when thickly smeared with
cooking fat. A similar experiment, with the rod whipped with
sticky horticultural tape, failed, as the tackiness served merely to
give a better grip. They were never satisfied, and if they arrived
when no food had been put out, ran sniffing over the ground;
poking their noses into the heap of hay, and finally, perplexed,
sat up on their hind legs staring incredulously at the empty feeding
ground. They then visited the bird tables and trays in turn, and
if these were found empty, leapt up on to the pergola roof where
they raided the wisteria buds—rough justice for those who had
failed to supply their needs.

The deer were lucky only if they arrived just after food was put
out. In theory it might appear easy to keep some always available
by putting down a continuous supply, but if I went out too often
to the feeding ground I was liable to meet the deer coming up the
garden. The fawn at least was never far off, and sometimes we
encountered one another.

The amount of food the deer enjoyed was considerable. I cut
up bushels of apples, mostly rough Cox and Bramley bought from
local orchards, and, as the native crop of sweet chestnuts had
failed, I was buying twelve-pound bags of Spanish chestnuts at
no little cost. A bagful would have been eaten every night if I
could have put one out. It was now December and there were
several months of feeding ahead as the deer were likely to come
habitually till the middle of the following April. I tried a variety of
food: brown bread, biscuit meal, flaked maize, sultanas, tinned
fruits, carrots and other root vegetables. They sniffed disdainfully
at everything, though I continued to present this selection on
several successive nights as I had noticed that a new food had to be
offered for some time before the deer would venture to try it. This
had happened with peanuts, which they now enjoyed.

# CHAPTER 6

---

# Born in Winter

28 DECEMBER 1965 brought a cold morning with sixteen degrees of frost. I went out early to feed the birds, and to break the ice on the ponds. On the way I saw three deer under the pines; the buck, doe, and fawn browsing together. But they were at once alerted and went off towards the water garden. This was my destination, but I made a tactical retreat, for the ice breaking could wait; the birds had other pools by the house. Later in the morning I crept out by another way, hoping to avoid disturbing the deer again. I broke the ice on the first pond and was moving to the next when I drew level with a low bush tangled in clematis bines—there was a sudden scuffle, and a spotted fawn ran out, almost from under my feet! It seemed little worried by the intrusion, and began at once to groom its coat, looking up occasionally to stare in my direction. It was, I thought, from two to three weeks old. The face, which appeared very small, was set in a ruffle of soft fur, for the whole pelage was dense and fluffy. It was dark brown but lighter on the underside and around the eyes, which intensified their brilliance; the nose was shiny and snub; the forehead high and well defined by the typical muntjac facial lines. The pelage was sombre in colour, and the spots indistinct, showing only at certain angles to the light, but some golden tone mingled with the brown of face and head, and lent a glow to the inner side of the neatly rounded ears. After a while, to my regret, the fawn stepped lightly through the undergrowth to disappear beneath a big overhanging laurel.

One felt that nature had blundered in bringing this tiny creature into the cold environment of winter. Vulnerable at all times, as a fawn must be in early life, it was born when little or no cover could be found; when the land was often chilled with snow and frost, or sodden with winter rain. Yet in this case mankind must take some of the blame having introduced these small Asiatic deer regardless of their ability to endure our climate. Muntjac fawns may be born at any time of year. I have records for January, March, April,

43

May, July, November and December. How many fawns survive the winter is not known. Few are found dead in the countryside, doubtless because foxes and other scavengers soon dispose of them. Some years ago a friend showed me one that had died in her garden during a spell of January snow. No more than a week or two old, it had known little but suffering as one of its hoofs had been severely injured early in life and the leg had withered. I made detailed studies of the pelage, which had pale cream spots clearly defined, and was lighter and more golden than in the one I had seen this morning.

The temptation to search for the new fawn was great, but if I penetrated the thicket into which it had gone, I was likely to disturb also the doe, who might then take it elsewhere. To be patient seemed the only course.

January brought another event when a new doe came to feed with the deer one evening. From her ready acceptance into the family circle I thought she was probably the fawn seen in the garden during 1964, as she appeared to be a young doe, an assumption that was proved later. As a fawn she had always been secretive, and we had not seen her for a long time. Though the weather was cold and snow was lying she did not seem hungry, and stood watching the others, occasionally taking a few leaves of *Asarum europaeum*, a plant which suffered some browsing as it was beside the feeding place, and apparently liked by the deer. When the buck and doe left, the young doe followed down the garden, where the three wandered amicably. I also came across her sometimes during the day, as she was sharing the territory.

On 4 January the new fawn came with the doe, and from then began to make frequent appearances. We now had five deer, and the attraction of the feeding ground allowed me to see the behaviour of a number together. That muntjac should come to feed in this way by the house, was something I had never thought possible. It was a great advance since the first intrepid approach of the buck two years ago.

This had not been achieved without some inconvenience, as our lives had to be adjusted to fit in with the deer's movements. Only by exerting great care could I take the car in and out at night without alarming the deer, and cars visiting other houses in the area caused a lot of disturbance after dark, partly through unnecessary engine revving and slamming of doors. It was tantalising

when this occurred while I was sketching, as it sent the deer off at once. They became accustomed to cars passing in the lane, about thirty yards from the feeding ground, but if one stopped, all heads were instantly raised; the deer stood poised for a second, then one took off, and the rest followed. There was a long wait before any returned.

Most of our visitors had been tactfully warned, and we avoided, when possible, dealing with tradesmen who delivered goods after dark. The roundsman's job seems to produce an exceptionally light-hearted character; filled with the joy of life, and whistling his way through all weather in stout, if not hob-nailed, boots. Deliveries from a certain London store were occasional but always seemed to coincide in winter with the deer's first feed. It was difficult to explain the position to a Londoner, whose conception of wild life was probably limited to a sparrow on the roof. Yet strangely the mention of deer had a magical effect—he went out like a mouse, as did the burly corn chandler on another occasion.

The import of food supplies for birds and deer created problems. No one could be expected to unload and deliver silently from a heavy lorry, and I had to stock large amounts to reduce deliveries

to a minimum. But wherever I tried to store the food it was raided by field-mice, whose ingenuity knew no bounds. They came up through incredibly small chinks in the floorboards of the shed, and gnawed through two layers of plastic bags in which I had previously thought the food secure. It seemed a losing battle when voles and even shrews joined the invaders.

The deer fed near to the main door of the house, and there was always a risk that someone would come through the garden gate, leading to it, when they were feeding. The gate had therefore to be kept bolted, and as a further insurance, a notice diverted everyone to the back door. All visitors, familiar and unfamiliar, were received at this door, which caused some embarrassment as it is difficult to keep the kitchen on the same plane of respectability as the hall. We avoided noise as much as possible, and I asked friends not to telephone after dark unless the call was urgent, as the bell frightened and bewildered all but the most tolerant of the deer.

Our freedom in the garden was also restricted and no work could be done or bonfires lit where deer were likely to be harbouring in adjacent thickets. Scything was banned in the wild garden as it deprived the deer of cover, consequently stinging nettles and other invasive weeds grew to rampant proportions, casting their seed far and wide.

Deer-watching occupied most of my evenings and a great deal of time, but it was an opportunity to study muntjac behaviour which could not be missed.

Names for wild animals, suggest a human guise incompatible with wild life, but without them, references to the two fawns were conflicting; the young buck became known as Little Fella, and the new fawn as Tiny.

It was interesting to note the selective fancies of individual deer. Coxes were the doe's first choice, with sweet chestnuts to follow, while another reversed this order, eating many chestnuts before turning to apple. They differed too in appetites; Little Fella seemed to have the greatest capacity, but the doe sometimes fed methodically for as long as half-an-hour. One can scarcely suppose Little Fella knew that by coming early he could gain a major share of his favourite food, but he was often first at the feast, and any deer coming after for conkers was likely to be unlucky, for he took them in scrambled haste and soon disposed of nearly all I had put out. Deer arriving later searched diligently but found few. Yet there was never any attempt by one deer to drive another from the food. In winter, feeding usually began about five p.m. and from then throughout the evening the deer fed at intervals, drifting away and returning to feed again. Sometimes one or more stayed for a time ruminating under the golden yew which was involved in the circle of light from the window, but when they went beyond this it was difficult to see what they were doing, though in moonlight their movements could be followed till they disappeared beyond the bushes or bamboo thickets.

In parts of the garden which the deer used frequently, they formed a maze of paths, with lairs in the undergrowth, in which they lay ruminating. Such haunts were used for a while but eventually deserted and others taken over. All tracks and signs such as these were interesting to translate into deer activity, and one could learn considerably from them, but to see the deer in person always added zest to observation. They came readily into the artificial light when used to it, and seemed very contented, feeding and grooming, or standing for a while contemplating the scene. If they heard another animal approaching they were at

once alerted and stood listening intently, almost sure it was one of the family, but not taking any chances. When this happened I hoped for the arrival of another deer, though sometimes it proved to be only a bustling hedgehog. This winter several had failed almost entirely to hibernate, and joined the deer on all but the coldest nights. It seemed strange to see them out in the snow.

In the past the study of hedgehogs had interested me keenly, but as the deer were likely to be encountered at any time from dusk onward it was impossible to go out to watch the hedgehogs without disturbing the deer. The bamboo thickets with their deep litter of palm-like leaves have long been an attraction to nesting hedgehogs, and I have had good watching and opportunities to sketch the young when they emerged from the nest, and on their nightly foraging with the adult. Now I had to be content with what I could see of hedgehog activity from the windows. This was often amusing, if not very informative. Four were coming to food put out for them near the deer's supper, but I had difficulty in keeping neighbouring cats from stealing it; bread-and-milk, cheese, and meat were all taken unless I put the dishes under cover. Ridge tiles make good tunnels into which hedgehogs will go readily if food is to be found inside. I had two of these, but the four hedge-hogs often arrived almost together, and those who had already laid claim to the tunnels were fiercely butted in the rear by their hungry competitors. There was frequent bickering among them, and disputes usually ensued between two feeding close together. The one who was getting the worst of the argument, eventually sought refuge by curling up. The aggressor then continued to bully the loser, and the rounded form rolled ahead down the slope, with the butting hedgehog scurrying after, puffing and pushing to speed it on its way.

Though the resort to curling up may at first seem expedient, with head tucked in, there is presumably no way of telling when it is safe to emerge. The rolled hedgehog usually waited for some minutes before venturing partly to unroll. If then the aggressor was still within striking distance, it took a hasty glance and shut to again. But if danger was past, quickly scrambled to its feet and scuttled away on short anxious legs to safety.

The belligerent manners of the hedgehogs contrasted sharply with those of the deer family. They fed side by side and friendly feeling among them was displayed in the rubbing of heads together, and grooming, one for another. There were sudden intervals of play, with the fawn cutting capers round the buck, and occasionally I saw him nuzzle the buck on the mouth as though trying to induce him to part with the chestnut he was eating. Such behaviour was seen only on still nights. During high winds the deer were usually very furtive, and feeding was accompanied by continual ear flicking as they strained to detect any signs of danger in the bewildering medley of sound. The ears could be turned almost completely backwards, and were sometimes used independently to guard against threats from different directions. On windy nights the food was snatched hastily, and a violent gust often sent the deer racing for cover.

The erection of lights on houses is a growing fashion as more townspeople come to live in the country. It seems alien to the countryside at night, though to comply with the townsman's wishes, street lighting is often imposed on lanes and commons where the countryman previously found no difficulty in seeing his way, even on the darkest nights.

Lamp-posts are a nuisance to the naturalist, particularly if he is unlucky enough to have one alongside his property. Light which cannot be switched off when necessary is a handicap to the study of wild life, as some animals are severely inhibited by it. But a light controlled by the watcher can sometimes be turned to advantage, as with the deer in the garden. I would have preferred not to use artificial light, but little could be seen without, as the deer's pelage merged almost completely into the dusk or darkness. When they had become conditioned to the light they seemed to ignore it, though I noticed robins and blackbirds in the vicinity going later than usual to their roosts, and early songsters were sometimes heard when the light was used before dawn. This made me hesitate to have more powerful lighting, but it was opportune as a temporary measure to enable me to see more detail for sketching, and I exchanged the original light for a spotlight reflector which could be directed from a flexible fitting.

The deer fed only a few yards from the windows, and to introduce them to the new light gradually, I fixed a small sheet of tissue paper over the pane immediately in front of the bulb to reduce its brilliance. In spite of this, I switched the light on for the first time in some trepidation, wondering if the deer would take exception to the change.

Little Fella arrived about five o'clock, and was soon followed by the buck and doe. To my relief none showed any reaction, and the buck and Little Fella, in playful mood, exchanged some friendly combat. Next evening I moved the paper screen, and the deer seemed not to notice the difference.

Evenings were very full with the family coming to feed, sometimes all together. Tiny, the new fawn, took little interest in the food, and spent her time leaping and scampering over the lawn with a vitality that was delightful to watch. Her sudden movements sometimes took even the buck by surprise, sending him off at speed if she came up behind him unexpectedly.

Here it will be noted that I have used the feminine gender for the fawn, though whether this was a male or female deer I did not know. The sex of young fawns is sometimes difficult to define in the field, and at this stage in my observations I decided to record all fawns as female till pedicles or other signs clearly indicated the sex as that of a young buck.

# CHAPTER 7

## Joy and Sorrow

THE sanctuary was again in the grip of winter with snowfall covering most of the deer's food supply. But they were coming for food put out, and several of the shelters were in use. They seemed to have few problems as their needs were always at hand. But one morning I found the tracks of a hungry fox across the garden, and feared for the new fawn, though it was not to her that tragedy came. The young doe who had joined the family in early January had not been seen at the feeding ground for a while, and I concluded she came when I was not watching, as I had seen her elsewhere in the garden several times, looking out from cover as I passed. But in the bitter weather that followed, we found her, lifeless and frozen under a thick laurel hedge, a leaf between her lips in a last effort to survive. She had been sorely stricken as one foot had been severed above the hoof, perhaps by a trap set somewhere beyond the garden for the wandering fox, or she may have leapt on to a broken bottle, its razor sharp edges hidden under the snow. It was distressing that we had not been aware of her plight, though there was little we could have done, except to leave food near places where she was seen lying-up. With such a handicap she could not have lasted long, and the severe weather hastened her end.

How much deer are affected by cold when in normal health one cannot tell. Judging by the long periods of inactivity they indulge in, at least during the day, their resistance must be good. They appeared happy enough at the feeding ground in times of frost and snow, and probably suffered more discomfort from heavy rain, when I have seen them looking very wet.

Tiny was now taking some of the food but her needs were small as she was not yet fully weaned. A dainty, swift little being, still very youthful though in many ways surprisingly mature. She groomed herself with all the agility of the adult, balancing on three legs while lifting the fourth to scratch a shoulder or any other demanding spot. Though she was often in the doe's company she

sometimes went away into the night alone looking very independent.

I realised my good fortune in being able to watch muntjac, shyest of deer, in this intimate way nightly. Before, my mammal study, whether of deer, fox, or badger, had entailed being out late in remote places, reached sometimes by stumbling long distances over ploughed fields and woodland in the dark, regardless of weather. But now the deer were giving arm-chair watching, in which their behaviour could be seen without effort. The extent to which they had made themselves at home was measured by the casual and often amusing behaviour that occurred incidental to feeding: the gentle caress, the buck playfully butting Little Fella in the rear when his table manners became too pushing; the head to head but friendly dispute between two nuzzling for food under the hay. There was generally no sense of hurry, and sometimes one or more would stand for a long time grooming or ruminating under the golden yew beside the feeding place.

The deer's reactions to disturbance varied with the degree of suspicion it created. If serious they leapt away with the speed of light, but if merely startled, perhaps by the unexpected arrival of another deer or a sudden gust of wind, the alert deer crouched immediately, lowering the body almost to the ground by rapidly flexing first the back legs then the front, there remaining, tense, ready for the leap to follow should the danger materialise. I have seen this action also as a part of playful combat among the deer.

Tiny was now about six weeks old, and her relationship with the doe was still very close. Together they were always fascinating to watch, and I saw many incidents of charm normally hidden from human eyes.

Anything new at the feeding ground always attracted Tiny. One evening she discovered several apples I had spiked on sticks to hold them rigid on the ground for the birds to peck. The game of getting one off the stick occupied her while the other deer fed, and she worried it repeatedly, leaving with obvious reluctance to follow the doe. It seems that even in the wild the unattainable fruit is sweetest.

Tiny was now becoming more venturesome. One morning early I saw her having a riotous game by herself; racing back and forth over the lawn, leaping high in ecstasy of joy. Suddenly she stopped, and wandered over to the feeding ground to nose under the hay, for it had not taken her long to learn that if food was not found elsewhere this was the place to look. A hen pheasant fed beside her, each apparently ignoring the other's company, and when Tiny had eaten she drifted away. On the lawn she encountered another pheasant, and on sudden impulse raced after her, taking to the air in long leaps that sent the pheasant scuttling for cover. As the fawn rounded a bush she came upon two more; they scrambled away almost taking wing, with Tiny hard on their tails, delighted

to find someone, even if unwilling, to join in the game. But her sudden leaps and turns of speed were too much for them and after a while they evaded her among the bushes. Presently I saw them creeping out on the other side, tip-toeing towards the feeding ground, though keeping a wary eye on the fawn. But she had lost interest, and suddenly, with a twinkle of her tail, was gone!

The comparative progress and behaviour of the two fawns of different ages was interesting to watch. A contrast was marked by the more staid disposition of Little Fella, whose playfulness was now only occasional, and the complete abandon often shown by Tiny, scampering in and out of the shadows; one moment hidden and the next, like a leaf caught in the wind, flicking into the light, then away!

Though the deer did not usually show any sign of recognition on meeting, I sometimes saw the buck and Little Fella rub noses in greeting—a message passed between them and was occasionally elaborated by the buck's caress. In spite of his strong masculine bearing, he often showed a surprising tenderness towards the young. He was bolder than the doe, who continued to display the instinctive caution of her sex. Any change in the landscape at the feeding ground caught her attention at once. A stone left out of the birds' pool when the water was changed, she regarded with deep suspicion. She sniffed it cautiously at a distance with head lowered, and creeping up to it slowly backed, then came forward again, finally walking past in a sideways gait, still watching the stone intently as though she expected it suddenly to come to life.

She was of gentle disposition and her attitude one of forebearance. The only time I saw her display any signs of annoyance was when the buck persisted in scenting her, a habit occasionally indulged in also by Little Fella. She showed her resentment by up-tailing and walking away; a measure that sometimes kept her from the food till the others had finished eating. Though she could have put Little Fella at least in his place she never attempted to do so.

All the deer looked in splendid condition. Their coats were glossy and sleek, with the high lights merging softly into the deep richness of tone as the sheen on watered silk. Each deer was distinct in character and I never saw one which could easily be mistaken for another. I made many chalk sketches at night, and also notes of colour. These I was able to record in detail from the young doe who died in winter—a depressing task, for I never enjoy sketching a dead animal or bird, but colour and other data so recorded are valuable to both artist and naturalist.

The deer were still taking a lot of food. They all eat heartily, but Little Fella was easily the champion. Tiny's appetite matched her small size; a few pieces of apple and a leaf or two of asarum were all she usually needed, then she was away, leaping over her black shadow in a sudden turn of mood. The others often stayed feeding for a long time. All were fond of peanuts, but for these there was competition from hedgehogs and field-mice. The buck had a special liking for the nuts, and on arrival searched the ground nose down, picking them up at lightning speed. He would have eaten

several pounds at a time but there had to be some limit. I had already bought a sackful for the birds and deer at the beginning of the season, expecting, as in previous winters one or two deer, and I had not provided for a family. My store of conkers and chestnuts was running out, and I was reduced to cutting the remaining few in half, and scattering them in an attempt to slow down the early comers and reserve some for deer who arrived later. Coxes were still preferred to cookers, and cut apple was sorted carefully to extract the sweet pieces first.

One evening I watched a delightful mock battle between Tiny and the buck; an example of training incorporated in play of the very young. After the family had fed, the buck wandered down to the lawn, followed by Tiny. Almost at once she began to play, running to the buck, who lowered his head inviting her to attack. Her diminutive blows were gently returned, and she came back many times, skipping round him, occasionally breaking off to disappear at speed beyond the bushes, but within seconds, leaping out again to do battle. The contest lasted for nearly ten minutes, then suddenly the demeanour of both changed. The buck paused to sweep his tongue across the fawn's head, and each turned aside in search of new interests.

This was a good time for watching a fawn, as the winter season brought the deer often to the food. Had she been a summer fawn I would have seen perhaps little of her at this early age. When foliage is thick a fawn may remain undiscovered for a long time. Little Fella had been born in April, and though I was fortunate in seeing him on and off through spring to summer, he had been older than Tiny when winter brought him to the feeding ground. Now at ten months he was a fine little buck in full vigour and health, with dense glossy coat and first antlers showing above the hairy pedicles. The two fawns were boon companions and family unity was strong, but I wondered how much longer the buck would tolerate Little Fella in his territory. It is known that young roe deer, born in May, are usually driven out by the next spring, and I hoped this would not happen with Little Fella, as I wanted to watch his progress if possible till maturity.

But life in the wild is always insecure. Species are designed to prey upon one another, and many animals die in infancy. Sadly, man is often the greatest predator. Protection is afforded to domestic animals but too often a blind eye is turned to suffering in

Pedicles

Velvet

Hard Horn

the wild, especially if it interferes with man's pleasure or monetary gain. There is too the cruelty that arises from thoughtless action. Broken glass and sharp edged tins are left in the countryside by picnic parties, and near some residential areas the woods become a dumping ground for every unwanted article. Discarded wire-netting, rotten sheet metal and other dangerous objects may cause injury and suffering among both wild and domestic animals. Traps too are a danger, not only to those for whom they are set, but to animals in general, as legislation, which forbids their being set in the open, is frequently disregarded. Such hazards should not be found in gardens, but the deer wandered farther afield, and one evening when Little Fella came to feed I saw to my dismay that he was standing with his front feet splayed, and was lifting first one then the other, resting each in turn. He eat little, and when he left, hobbled painfully across the lawn. It was obvious that his feet were injured.

I waited anxiously next evening wondering if he would come, but saw only the doe. By morning all the food had gone, though whether he had been among the feeding deer I could not tell. The following night I watched for him again, yet feeling he was probably lying-up somewhere with his feet too painful for even a short journey. The doe came twice between six and seven o'clock, then I had a long wait while, strangely, no deer were seen. The night had been quiet, without any disturbance; no visitors, no ringing telephone bell, and I wondered what could be keeping the deer away. But shortly before ten o'clock I went up to my bedroom window to get a wider view across the garden, and almost at once saw the cause of the trouble—well lit in the floodlight, a man was creeping along the pergola. He stopped to peer into the room where my sister was reading, blissfully unaware of his company! The nature of his mission was obvious from the proverbial iron bar he was clutching. I fled downstairs to give warning, then to the phone to dial 999! This was a mistake in the interest of deer watching; within ten minutes a bevy of police were ranging the garden with powerful torches, and the deer doubtless fleeing in terror!

The burglar, who had meanwhile employed himself breaking and entering, fled along the lane. But a constable was hard on his heels, having vaulted the five-foot gate (topped by wire netting to confuse marauding cats) to sieze him as he reached for the starter button of his elegant sports car!

I saw no more of the deer that night, but between return visits of the police, which went on till the early hours, a hedgehog, self-possessed as usual, took a lone supper.

After a few nights Little Fella returned. It was a relief to see him again, but his feet showed no improvement, and I could see the marks of injury just above the hoofs. He looked furtive and unhappy, and the scent glands below the eyes were open, indicating fear and probably pain. But nature sometimes shows remarkable powers of healing, and there was still hope of his recovery. If he remained in the garden, and he seemed unlikely to go far, he should be safe from predators, but his speed was seriously impaired, and if attacked his chances of escape would be slender.

# CHAPTER 8

# The Killers

THE doe had no hesitation in bringing her young near the house, and one afternoon I saw her suckling Tiny at a short distance from the windows. The fawn was then about nine weeks old and taking apple and peanuts chosen from the food I put out. I cut the apples mostly into small pieces for her benefit but she usually nosed among them to find the biggest. These presented a problem as she could keep them in her mouth only by tossing her head back repeatedly to retain them till they were chewed to manageable size. She had not yet attempted the chestnuts, which were presumably too hard. About this time I noticed the adult deer going to the birds' pool to drink. I had not seen them drinking before, but it became almost a regular habit except during wet weather.

There was still no sign that Little Fella was being driven out of the family circle. Friendly feeling seemed general among the deer, and was not confined to relations between those of opposite sex. Sometimes Little Fella was seen fondling the doe, but it was not unusual for him to nuzzle the buck's face, and receive a gentle grooming in return. Their actions seemed entirely natural in spite of human proximity.

Meals were sometimes interrupted by causes unheard and unseen from the house, but if the disturbance was slight, the deer soon returned. Generally all left if one was alerted, though the boldest might delay to snatch a coveted piece of food on the way.

March began with Tiny's introduction to chestnuts, which she was now able to chew, rejecting the shucks as neatly as did the adults. It was surprising that such hard food could be managed at this early age.

Little Fella was still troubled by his injured feet, though they were improving slowly, and on one occasion I saw him run for a short distance across the lawn. But it was unlikely that he would ever regain the speed normally enjoyed by deer. Though muntjac are of heavier build than some species, they can if alarmed get

61

away very quickly, leaping straight up from the ground, to disappear almost faster than the eye can follow. One windy night a sudden gust sent the buck and Tiny from the food, one left!—one right! and I scarcely saw their going. They stopped as suddenly a few yards away, aware that they had been tricked by the wind, and came back to feed.

Since the injury to his feet, Little Fella had always appeared furtive and ill at ease. He rarely fed by the house in daylight, though not infrequently the buck and Tiny joined the pheasants in the early morning. On their arrival most of the birds retired to a respectful distance, where, craning their necks, they stood anxiously peering from behind the bushes before venturing to return. If the deer came first, arriving pheasants froze in their tracks on seeing them. All heads came up to stare, till presently the bolder members of the troop approached with caution to feed beside them. The rest waited till the deer had gone, then ran like scurrying chickens to the feast. But in time most of the birds became accustomed to sharing their meal with the deer, and the tamest pheasant, who sometimes fed from my hand, allowed Tiny to come up close beside her. All was well unless the pheasant chanced to move suddenly. This was a signal to the fawn for play, and she leapt at once after her. She fled in haste but Tiny was not easily put off once her spirit of fun was alerted, and the pheasant found herself an unwilling partner in a game which was to her of doubtful merit.

As we neared the end of March I felt that the lure of food would not hold the deer much longer, and wondered if a salt lick would prove attractive. When watching deer in woodland a few years ago I had tried one with limited success. I had also put some on a stub beside a deer path in the garden from time to time, though it was never touched. Their interest in one by the feeding ground was very slight, but aroused their curiosity. The buck saw it first, and stretching out his head sniffed cautiously, but dismissed it as inedible and therefore worthless. The doe was even more careful. She halted in her tracks, and stood for some minutes staring at it, with a puzzled expression, one ear up, the other down. She crept nearer, sweeping her head from side to side, as a suspicious badger emerging from the sett, then sniffed long and deliberately and turned away. Next evening she made a further inspection, viewing it warily, but after this her interest waned and it was ignored.

# The Killers

Later when the buck was renewing his antlers I tried again, as at this time deer are in need of mineral salts, which may be lacking in their diet, but I had no success.

As I continued to study the deer, I found the ability to recognise individuals increasingly helpful. One could connect the happenings, as those involved in the breeding cycle and regrowth of antlers, with particular deer. It was especially valuable if observation could be continued, as I hoped with Little Fella, for a long period. But a cloud of insecurity hung over the young buck, and I felt that either way, whether by impending disaster through the weakness due to his injured feet, or through the natural cause of independence as he matured, I would not have much longer to record his progress.

April came with brilliant skies, great clouds ranging high and fast over the blue; sudden showers, and sunlight almost before they had passed; clear drops on every twig; the air clear and refreshed. Then, the singing is without pause, and the industry of life involves even the smallest creatures. Yet at mid-day there is a slackening of effort when for a short time the birds relax to preen and sunbathe; mammals are mostly in hiding; deer lying-up in thickets, half asleep.

But danger lurks in the wild at all times. It was during this lull that I suddenly heard the cries of a deer. The muntjac call is harsh and to human ears has an element of distress. But this was indicative of extreme anguish, and as I ran down the garden I heard also the sharp savage barking of dogs. Two ran off as I came on the scene, but they had already done their work. Little Fella lay struggling in the hollow of a ditch where they had attacked him. In the few minutes I had taken to reach him, they had inflicted terrible injuries. Gaping wounds scored his back and legs; his belly was torn apart, but he tried desperately to rise, though, as we learned later, his pelvis was broken.

Animals are often strangely quiet in pain, and we found that if we were out of sight the cries ceased, but he continued from time to time the struggle to get to his feet. His condition was hopeless and we could do nothing but watch to prevent the dogs from returning till veterinary help could give him release. It is sad that such help must for wild animals add further terror through human contact.

The gradually weakening cries as the drug took effect, were indicative of the trail of suffering the dogs had left in their wake, for

63

it was proved later that they had been ranging the countryside killing and maiming other animals unchecked for months.

People who allow their dogs to roam often inflict great cruelty on other animals, wild and domestic. There is no more delightful companion than the dog, but when he is permitted to run free he usually reverts in a short time to savage tendencies. He induces others to join forces, and they spend their time hunting in the countryside where, once they have developed the lust to kill, they destroy almost any defenceless animal that crosses their path. Among a litter of fox cubs I was watching in the area, one lay dead near the earth, and another had been severely mauled. After a few nights it disappeared. A mile or so away a farmer had lost forty-two sheep through savaging by dogs which had so far not been caught. It was significant that two answering the description of those that came to the sanctuary had been seen ranging his fields on a number of occasions. A glance at the figures for sheep and other stock worrying supplied by U.F.A.W. shows how widely this occurs. In one year, typical of annual returns, there were 3,350 cases of sheep worrying in England and Wales, resulting in 2,723 animals killed, and 3,870 injured. Poultry worrying caused the deaths of nearly 8,000 birds, and 1,419 injured. These figures do not take into account many cases not reported by farmers.

The situation is particularly bad around new towns and housing estates where many people come to live in the country for the first time and have no regard for the country code, often scarcely knowing of its existence. They adopt a dog as a family pet and in mistaken kindness allow it to roam to its heart's content. Very soon it is out of control and becomes a rabid killer, though it may remain gentle and loveable in the home. Farmers, gamekeepers and certain other landowners can legally shoot on sight any animal found worrying their stock, and eventually the dog will pay the price, but not till he has inflicted great suffering.

I wondered if there would be any visible reaction among the deer to the loss of Little Fella. The first night the food was scarcely touched, and I did not see any of the deer. But during the following evening the buck put in a brief appearance, though most of the food was left. The next night, he came twice, but no deer were seen on the following night. I had not encountered the doe or Tiny since the tragedy, and anxiety for their safety increased. The killers were still at large as we had not so far been able to trace hem. But next morning the buck was seen taking food early and he came again in the evening. I kept a long watch at the window, and to my relief saw Tiny emerge from the shadows to feed. She began to come regularly again, but a fortnight passed before the doe was seen. She appeared to have lost some of her former confidence, and did not stay long. No certain conclusions can of course be drawn from this, though, as a cow obviously grieves for her calf, it is reasonable to suppose that deer are similarly affected. It is always difficult to assess the feelings of animals, or to know the extent of psychological disturbance caused by their witnessing or hearing the anguish of one of their own kind. We are left wondering.

Tiny was now lying-up by day under a berberis bush not far from the house; hidden from view behind the dense prickly branches that formed a secluded canopy. As I watched her disappearing under it I felt frustrated, wondering what she did in her lair during the day. When Little Fella had lain under the currant bushes, I noticed that he appeared to rest through most of the daylight hours, but I wanted more detail of activity, and hopefully erected a bracken shelter under the birches, at a short distance from the windows. I thought it was probably too near for occupation, but one morning looked out to see Tiny comfortably installed. Though this was mid-April, we had an unwelcome fall of snow,

heavy enough to flatten the daffodils and other early flowers, and to bring many shrubs to the ground. This uncomfortable weather doubtless prompted Tiny to find a dry lair, and as the shelter faced towards the windows, I was able to record her movements. The following extracts from my diary of that time are typical:

| | | |
|---|---|---|
| 17 April | 9 a.m. | Tiny in her lair. |
| | 11 a.m. | Out to feed and wander. |
| | 3 p.m. | She has come back. |
| | 7.20 p.m. | Out, taking herbage, then away. |
| | | |
| 18 April | 6 a.m. | Tiny in her lair again. |
| | 8.45 a.m. | Still there and grooming. I opened a window and looked out. She lifted her head and stared but did not move. Grooming again. She curls her long tongue around her nose from one side to the other, and is even able to reach her eyes. |
| | 3 p.m. | She came out to eat a little herbage and some apple, then back into lair. |
| | 7.20 p.m. | She has gone. |
| | | |
| 19 April | 6.20 a.m. | Tiny came to the feeding ground, had a meal of apple, chewed a chestnut, then returned to her lair. |
| | 11.15 a.m. | I put food out for her under the yew, but she was alerted and left. |
| | 12 noon | She returned to feed, and went back to shelter. |
| | 7.45 p.m. | She grooms her coat frequently. Out and away. |
| | | |
| 20 April | 6.20 a.m. | Tiny came for apple, then went into lair, taking leaves of ivy and Welsh poppy on the way. |
| | 12 noon | Out for more apple, but rain started, and she returned to the shelter. |
| | 6.30 p.m. | Tiny out again. She took a little food then back to lair. |
| | 7.45 p.m. | Out for the night. |

## The Killers

From these notes it is seen that during most of the day she was lying up in cover, but came out at intervals for snacks. Sometimes she lay with her head resting across her back legs, dozing and occasionally looking out at the weather, or yawned with almost human boredom. Much of her time was spent grooming; going over her coat carefully with her tongue, and it was easy to see why the deer always looked scrupulously clean and immaculate.

When the weather became milder she used the lair in the shelter less, though she may have been lying-up in another. I usually avoided going near the shelters, specially those in thickets where one had to be very close to see whether they were in use. One day when carrying a bundle of bedding to a shelter which I thought was unoccupied (I had seen spiders' webs across the entrance recently) I glimpsed the tip of Tiny's ear just in time, and withdrew hastily, unseen and unheard. It was a long time before I ventured to call there again.

The deer still came for food through April and May; sometimes in the early morning but more often from dusk onward. In June their visits were infrequent, though I met Tiny sometimes in the garden, and she returned to the bracken shelter near the house in mid-June.

I supplied food during the summer (though there was no shortage in the wild) as I wanted to observe the deer, particularly the buck, and hoped to see when he cast his antlers, also to learn the time taken for renewal. Yet it was generally Tiny who came,

F

and her slots were found by the food whenever the ground was soft enough to retain them. She often fed with the hedgehog though it occasionally startled her by rustling out from cover unexpectedly. But they were on amicable terms and fed almost nose to nose. She watched the hedgehog's movements closely as it busted around looking for peanuts; mice too created a mild interest. She was now seven months old, and her coat was smoother in texture, having lost the early fluffiness of the first pelage. But at this age she was no less attractive as, daintily poised, she flicked the fallen rose petals from the grass with her tongue, and sipped from the moonlit pool.

The deer are pleasant to have in the sanctuary, and very clean in their habits. They have lavatories among the bushes, to which they retire, and none is used for more than a limited time. As vegetarians they do not interfere with other animals and one never comes across those distressing moments of the kill, which must sometimes be witnessed in association with carnivores. This is the normal course of nature, but it is not pleasant to observe, especially when the scales are weighted heavily in favour of the attacker, as between stoat and rabbit.

The stoat, a beautiful but relentless little killer, represents, for small mammals, the most deadly of predators, and the manner of its killing is indeed sinister. But whether in fact it is able to mesmerise its victims as alleged is open to doubt, and disbelieved by some reliable naturalists. Howard Lancum regards it as purely mythical and suggests that the rabbit's inability to realise that it can run from its tormentor is created by the paralysis of intense fear.

This part of the stoat's hunting, if it occurred, was hidden from me when, enjoying the woods in autumn, I strolled back to my car, along the ride. I was suddenly aware of violent movement ahead: a stoat and rabbit, breaking cover from the undergrowth, were grappling in the open. The rabbit was struggling in a last desperate effort to free itself from the attacker whose teeth were already deeply imbedded in the back of its neck. Its struggles were soon over. It lay still, paralysed by the bite, which had probably penetrated the spinal cord. The stoat, its blood lust not yet satisfied, bit savagely again and again into the face of the helpless rabbit. Pausing for a moment it looked up and saw me standing on the ride. It slid quickly into the undergrowth, and when after a while it did not return, I walked on to the scene of the kill. As I reached the rabbit I saw that it was still breathing; the soft fur on its breast rose and fell rhythmically, as it stared at me in the extremity of fear. Hoping to lessen this, I moved out of its direct line of vision. Presently I saw the stoat watching me with piercing eyes from the bracken at the edge of the ride. It advanced, hesitated, came almost to my feet, then scurried back. In a few minutes it was out again, and growing bolder went to the rabbit, sniffing, and undulating over and around it, but, still acutely aware of the watcher, stared balefully at me, and ran again into cover.

Whether the rabbit was now conscious I could not tell; the fur on its breast was still gently pulsating. It seemed the merciful course to leave and let the stoat finish its deadly work.

# CHAPTER 9

# Into Summer

JULY brings a sense of leisure to the wild. Young birds now strong on the wing are fending for themselves; cubs gaining their independence. The ceaseless efforts of spring are rewarded in sunlit days; darkness still and scented, cooled by heavy dew.

But this mood was not for the deer. Suddenly, the nights, which had been silent, echoed to their barking—provocative, loud and persistent—challenging—growing fainter, returning and again arresting—the call of running deer!

The rutting season was in full swing, and daylight showed many newly trodden paths formed by the deer in nuptial chase—through the long grass; around thorn bushes and scrub; down the slope to the water garden, encircling groups of wild flowers and saplings— back through the wood—there a check, and again the wild glad calls!

Two more nights of abandon, then silence.

At this time the deer were harbouring in a shubbery on adjacent land, from where a neighbour had seen them emerge sometimes in the evenings. It was a strange choice as she kept a number of small dogs. Though well behaved, they were always let out late for a last run in the garden, a ritual which was usually accompanied by much high pitched squealing and yapping, typical of the papillon breed. One night, hearing an additional commotion, the owner went out to investigate. Realising that an argument was taking place between her pets and the deer, she called the dogs to her, and picking one up, started back to the house. Looking over her shoulder she was astonished to find herself pursued by the angry buck; anxious and resentful at this intrusion of his territory, and showing the typical boldness of deer in general at rutting time.

About a fortnight later the same neighbour was rewarded by the pleasure of seeing a very young fawn in her garden with the doe. This was doubtless born shortly before the rut and probably contributed to the buck's belligerent and protective mood.

With a firm date for rutting, I hoped to be able to obtain the date of birth for the next fawn, which in turn would give the length of time between the two events. But the ways of deer are so unpredictable that I scarcely dared to hope that this piece of knowledge would come my way.

During August some of the deer came for food almost nightly. For the first week only the doe and Tiny were seen, but it was not long before the buck appeared, and I saw that he had recently cast his antlers. I had for a long time been hoping to learn more about antlers in muntjac, and this promised to be an opportunity. If the buck continued to come I would be able to note how long he remained in velvet, and the time taken from casting to hard horn. I watched anxiously for his return but three weeks passed without my having even a glimpse of him. Then one night, to my disappointment, a new buck arrived; a buck in hard horn, with the right antler deformed, and the ear on the same side mutilated. From this I assumed he had been injured while his antlers were growing and soft. Now in hard horn he had apparently taken possession of the territory while the rightful buck, having cast his antlers, was unable to defend it.

In about ten days the new buck came again to the feeding ground, and I saw no more of the buck of the two previous years. Whether he had, as I suspected, been driven out, or had met with disaster I could not tell. Possibly it is usual for muntjac to change doe and territory from time to time.

It is certain that all do not cast their antlers at the same season. Though the garden buck had cast in August, a friend living some distance away, reported seeing a buck in velvet in March, and one June evening when I was out badger watching, a buck who had recently cast his antlers strolled by within a stone's throw of my hiding place.

Seasonal changes of territory are also a phase in the muntjac's yearly cycle, as with many mammals. This is a feature of badger behaviour: often a colony has a sett in which it spends the winter and spring, but during summer one may watch there in vain, as the badgers have gone to an outlying sett; often beyond standing crops and therefore inaccessible to the watcher. This allows the main sett and its surroundings to freshen. Changes in the use of paths also take place from time to time, when those in current use around a sett are suddenly abandoned, and another series comes into use. The most likely explanation is that the badgers have found a new source of food which takes them on a different course. Similar behaviour is seen in muntjac territory when sanctuaries and paths previously in occupation, no longer show signs of activity. Another sanctuary is adopted, and fresh paths become indented with slots.

Unfortunately the deer of the garden sometimes make a change which involves the use of paths leading out across the lane which is narrow and winding, with steep banks on either side. The risk from traffic is obvious, and the buck had probably received his injuries on this or some other road. Muntjac are not infrequently killed through habitual crossing of roads. My request to the R.A.C. for a CAUTION DEER CROSSING sign, as used in the New Forest, was well received but frustrated by the County Council. When in the following year they erected a thirty m.p.h. sign farther down the lane, they left the narrowest part unrestricted.

The deer still use the route periodically, and it is always a relief when they revert to another in which they tend to keep mostly to field and garden. As I learned more about muntjac I found that change affected many aspects of their lives and behaviour. In the garden, habit brings them to the feeding ground over long periods from dusk onward, but occasionally for no apparent reason they come less during the evenings, and more often in the early morning. This continues for a while, then they return to the more usual hours. Similarly their appearances about the garden in daylight occur over periods, when it is not unusual to encounter them during the day. This may persist for a week or two, and has been noted also by a friend who has deer visiting her garden in another part of the county. I have had some of my best views of deer at play during these daylight periods, when two indulge in lively games; crouching face to face; suddenly leaping up and away, racing off at speed to disappear from sight, but almost at once returning in a wild chase; crouching again, and again bucking, leaping, tumbling over one another with the exuberance of playful puppies.

I have seen this play only among young deer and in common with other daylight behaviour it has occurred in the garden in phases, though whether it takes place among adults, and is a frequent part of muntjac behaviour I cannot say. These spells of daylight activity do not seem to occur in any particular season or climatic conditions, and not necessarily at the same time as

those noted elsewhere.

I saw little of the deer in October 1966, and they did not come during that month for food, though fresh slots were found every day in the garden, showing that they had been active there overnight. It was not till the beginning of November that the doe and Tiny returned to feed by the house. The buck soon followed. Meanwhile I had installed an additional light, which shone more directly on the deer from above and gave better vision down the garden. They now began to come regularly, though they took little food. If this continued over the winter the large quantities I had stored would not be wanted. During the autumn I had collected a hoard of conkers and sweet chestnuts; a task which took much time and effort, and the summerhouse was stacked with bushels of apples. All these items had been acceptable to the deer and eaten with relish throughout the last winter and spring. Now they looked the menu over with indulgence, casually taking a few peanuts, as the fancy willed—the delicious Coxes, the sweet chestnuts, and the conkers remained uneaten on the ground.

The early winter was mild, and herbage, more plentiful than usual at this time, probably had a greater appeal than any food I could offer.

During the second week in December, Smallest, the fawn of the past July, came with the doe and Tiny, and was soon as frequent in her visits as the rest of the family. At night the company included hedgehogs, rabbits, and long-tailed field-mice, all watched

74

intently by the fawn. The mice came out from a bank alongside to snatch peanuts almost from under her nose. Their movements were timed to a split second, competing even with those of the leaping fawn, whose neat little hoofs appeared each time to be aimed precisely on target yet always missed as the mouse in one leap reached the cover of the grassy bank. The other deer had long given up the hope of outwitting them, and after a while Smallest too learned to ignore their scurrying.

The snow and frost of early January cut down much of the wild herbage, and the deer became more interested in the food put out. The family party comprised four deer: the buck, the doe, Tiny and Smallest, who was now six months old. Though she enjoyed some of the food, on one occasion I saw her attempt to suckle from the doe, and concluded she was not yet fully weaned.

During the first week in January, I was able to make an addition to my notes on muntjac vocabulary. Though the buck and doe seemed always on good terms, from time to time the buck became very annoying, persistently scenting the doe while she was feeding. She usually evaded him by walking away without protest, but one evening seemed particularly irritated by his behaviour. Flicking her tail up, she emitted a shrill squeak, which, as his persistence increased, was extended to a series of rapid squeals syncronised each time with the lift of her tail. Finally she became so exasperated that she left the feeding ground. The buck then turned his attentions to Tiny, but she too up-tailed and with the same protesting squeals walked away. This solved a mystery, for I had sometimes heard this shrill call under my bedroom window, though till now it had been unexplained.

Muntjac are not generally vociferous, and apart from the raucous bark, which can be heard over a long distance, their conversation is carried on in muted tones. One must be close to hear the curious castanet call, which I had noted sometimes when deer were running through the undergrowth.

During the week when the squeaking was heard there were other signs of excitement among the deer. In several places on the lawns I found large, heavily indented slots and marks of sliding as though the buck had been indulging in skittish behaviour. Perhaps his thoughts were turning to the rutting season, though the doe could not be expected to show interest in such matters when she was, as later events proved, no more than seven weeks from the birth of a new fawn.

Tiny's appearances now became less frequent. She disappeared, at least from my view, for a week at the end of February, and I wondered if the doe was attempting to send her out of the territory as the arrival of her fawn was not far away. Unfortunately I did not see the behaviour of the two together at this time, though Tiny and the buck met sometimes at the feeding ground, and exchanged a nose to nose greeting. I also saw the buck fondling her.

The disappearance of each fawn in turn was one of the most tantalising aspects of my deer watching. In Tiny's case she had doubtless gained her independence, as she was over a year old. She had grown into a beautiful young doe. Her coat was exceptionally glossy and sleek, and she now had the white of the adult pelage on chin, neck, and chest, and under the belly. Her ears were neatly fringed on the inner edge with snow white fur, and the fluting or ridges were more deeply formed than on the ears of the original doe. It was interesting to compare her pelage with that of Smallest, six months old, which had no white except under the tail.

## Into Summer

Now, apparently without her playfellow, Smallest was looking for company. We had fifteen hen pheasants coming to feed, and one morning fawn and pheasants arrived together on the lawn. The fawn was in teasing mood. In seconds she was leaping among them, chivvying them around the shrubs as they ran for cover. They were soon hustled out again, and, near to losing their dignity, chased back across the lawn and around the birds' pool, with the fawn running and skipping behind. Lively and capricious she leapt in joyous take-off over their bewildered heads as they scattered in small groups before her, making once more for the cover of surrounding bushes. They could of course have taken wing, but while this game of tip-and-run was not a pastime they would have chosen, they were not disposed to leave without their breakfast on the lawn.

I was keeping a close watch on the doe, and saw her every night, but she was missing on 29 March, and I did not see her again till 2 April, when it was obvious from her slim appearance that she had dropped her fawn.

I now had certain dates for rutting and consequent birth of the fawn. The rutting had occurred between 11 and 14 July, and the fawn's birth eight-and-a-half months later. This period of time for gestation supported my previous records for which I had to rely on spells of vigorous barking occurring over several successive nights in or near the garden as evidence of rutting. The deer were usually quiet, and barking when heard was isolated and appeared to be a means of occasional communication, or caused by disturbance. I discredited more distant barking lest it was made by deer from other territory, though there was no sign of any in the immediate neighbourhood. In each instance, the sighting of a spotted or slightly older fawn had followed the event. Very young fawns had been seen generally eight to nine months after the assumed rut.

Following the birth of the fawn at the end of March, the buck showed a frequent desire to scent the doe when they were together at the feeding ground. I had not seen her there for several nights, and she appeared hungry, but he continued to worry her, and she soon left. When he had gone, she crept back through the bushes to feed alone, but after a while he returned, and she ran off pursued. In a few minutes I heard deer barking farther down the garden. Smallest, who had come to feed meanwhile, listened intently with

77

head up and much flicking of ears.

The next evening the buck was again very attentive, and as before, the doe responded by giving the shrill call. This behaviour occurred soon after the birth of the fawn, and barking, heard mostly in the early morning, between 2 and 8 April, also indicated rutting.

Since the arrival of the new fawn I had been hoping to come across it, but by 9 April I was no nearer than the finding of small slots beside the thicket where I had first encountered Tiny as a fawn. But a further search revealed others along a path leading to the wood, where the fawn had made a tour involving several of the deer's runways. Later in the morning I made another search, and suddenly found myself within a few paces of the fawn where it lay under a wild rose bush, its spotted golden-brown pelage flecked with sunlight. As it watched me, alert, ears pricked, I noted the small nose, delightfully snub; the high forehead and the dark lines of the facial ridges arched above the eyes giving it a look of innocent inquiry. I wondered what was passing through the mind of this quaint little being, scarcely more than a week old, as it stared out upon the vision of light and colour that met its ingenuous gaze.

When I returned, it was still undisturbed, and in the afternoon, by chance, looking out of a window, I saw the doe, followed by the buck, come through the wood to the rose bush and bring the fawn out to suckle in the open. The three wandered for a while among the hazels, and presently, to my regret, vanished beyond a thicket.

## Into Summer

Next morning the fawn was not in its accustomed place, and heavy rain had washed all tracks away. When after three days none was found I became anxious. Disaster could easily intervene at this early age. But in a short time I found the little slots again, and soon came across them over a wider area. I then began to encounter the fawn wandering in the early morning before it settled down for the day, and later it adopted the lair under the currant bushes as others had in the past. One morning we almost met, and for some minutes stared at one another. But in an unguarded moment I glanced away, and when I looked back the little clearing where it had stood was empty.

# CHAPTER 10

# From Velvet to Hard Horn

I CONTINUED to see the fawn in the garden, and one morning, early, put up the doe leaping before me over the wild parsley to a thicket, where she at once began to bark. I knew then that the fawn was hidden somewhere in the undergrowth, as the deer did not usually bark if disturbed in this way. Fear for the safety of the young accounts for many isolated periods of barking, though often if a deer gives voice for a short time the reason is unexplained, as one rarely has the good fortune to see a deer calling. One morning when I was watching Smallest feeding below my bedroom window, she suddenly indulged in a short spell of barking which lasted long enough for me to make a quick sketch before she continued her meal unconcerned. Why she had called I was unable to tell.

The fawn was nearly five weeks old when I first saw her come to the feeding ground with the doe. She went at once to the food as though used to coming, and I felt that I had probably missed earlier visits. She had grown rapidly, but her spots were still clearly visible, mainly in one long line from shoulder to tail, with the rest scattered in short broken lines. Freckles seemed an appropriate name.

The next time I saw her she was feeding with Smallest, and after this she began to come regularly with the doe. In colour they nearly matched as the doe was now in summer pelage.

The deer were not coming to feed as often as in winter, for May is a month of plentiful herbage. But even in June they were still attracted to the few out-of-season items I was able to offer. They came too for the fallen petals of *Magnolia Soulangiana*. These were much enjoyed by Smallest, who whipped them up rapidly with her tongue one after another from the grass.

There were too, moments of unexpected pleasure when I came upon the deer without their being aware of company; occasions which are perhaps those of greatest charm in watching any wild animal, as behaviour is then entirely natural. I was walking one evening, too early I thought to encounter deer, yet suddenly in a clearing under the pines, a mere twenty to thirty paces away, I saw the doe browsing from a hedge, and near her the fawn drifting through the grass; both were too engaged to notice my arrival. I crouched down behind some convenient bushes, and presently crept away, as the doe was moving towards me.

I did not see the buck often at this time though I found his slots in the garden daily, and sometimes beside those of the doe at the feeding ground. When he was seen, on 13 June, he had cast his antlers; an event of importance for my records. In a little over a week the new antlers had started to grow and were just visible. After about ten days, when he appeared again, they were approximately one-and-a-half inches long and showing very short brow tines. The velvet was glossy blue-grey above the gold of the hairy pedicles.

I hoped now to see him at intervals and to record the time taken from casting to renewal and hard horn. Every night I watched till late, and after I had gone to bed roused myself through the early hours to look out of my bedroom window hoping to see him feeding below. I had installed a switch beside my bed to control one of the lights.

With the deer now making only casual visits to the food, even intensive watching brought limited reward, but I persisted in my long vigils at the window. These were enlivened by the long-tailed field-mouse, *Apodemus sylvaticus*. A pair were frequenting a thick tangle of *Clematis montana* at the end of the pergola roof, from where they emerged at dusk to spend the early part of the evening scurrying along the beams and about the wisteria. Occasionally one stopped to sit up and nibble a minute portion of food held between the paws, possibly scraps of nut left by the tits, who often took food up there from the trays and tables below. After a time I found that the mice were venturing on to a hanging tray outside the window close to the light, which seemed not to worry them. The plump female, was entirely at her ease, and it was fascinating to watch the mice climbing at incredible speed up and down the wires that suspended the feeding tray. They travelled hand over hand or by keeping the paws together, in a series of rapid upward jerks. The two came for food every night and one evening the female was joined by a minute replica, very self-assured, on the tray beside her. After a time the young mice began to appear in twos and threes, and their antics on the wires were comical and

entertaining to watch, for they scrambled up and down even faster than the adults. After feeding they usually sat for a while washing their faces, passing their tiny paws over nose and whiskers as a hare in the field. They were nicely placed for sketching, which passed the time while waiting for the deer, and all became accustomed to my movements at the window. I was tempted to encourage them, and put out peanuts nightly; this was nearly their undoing. One evening when a young mouse was feeding, there was a silent flutter of wings, and a tawny owl alighted on the tray. In a flash the mouse was gone, escaping because it happened to be under the wire grid kept over one end of the tray to reserve food for small birds. Defeated, the owl swept up to perch on top of a conifer well lit in the beam of light. I watched it for some time as it surveyed the area, turning its head to stare around, presumably looking for moths and other small winged prey, many of which could be seen flying across the light. After this I saw the owl on a number of occasions watching from the conifer and from other perches within the area of light. In spite of its presence the field mice flourished, and sometimes came to the tray even in daylight. The first young were seen in June and were followed by successive litters through the year till mid-December—a poor prospect for our crocus species, the corms of which rarely escape some depredation.

From early July I waited eagerly for the return of the buck but did not see him again till 26 July, six weeks after he had cast his antlers. They had grown to approximately four inches, and the velvet was now brownish with pure grey only on the points. I found his slots during the coming week, and at the beginning of August saw him again when his antlers appeared about an inch longer and were slightly curved at the tips. After another week there was no marked difference, but on 19 August shrinkage of the velvet was visible at the points. The curves were more clearly defined as the velvet was now thinner, and I saw that the right antler, which had been damaged last season, was more acutely

23 June
10 days from casting

3 July
3 weeks from casting

26 July
6 weeks

5 August
7 weeks

24 August
10 weeks
velvet shrinking

6 September
12 weeks
velvet thin
antlers clean at tips

13 weeks
clean

curved at the extremity than the left. Apart from this both were well formed.

Ten weeks after casting, the velvet had shrunk considerably and the small brow tines were cleaning. I saw him also on 29 August and 1 September when he came in daylight. The velvet was beginning to look ragged, and on his next visit, four days later, the points were clean, though some velvet remained on the lower half of the antlers.

In the early hours and again at daybreak on 12 September, (thirteen weeks from casting) I heard barking in and near the garden. Unfortunately I could not see the barking deer, though I thought it was probably the buck in .challenging mood, as his antlers were now hardened and his old confidence returned.

Freckles had not been seen since the end of August, and after our last meeting I did not come across her slots again. She was then barely six months old, and it seemed possible she had wandered to outlying woods and fallen a victim to marauding dogs. There had been no sign of Smallest since mid-June, and one after another the fawns, apart from Little Fella whose fate was known, had vanished without trace.

Following what I thought was the buck's display of barking on 12 September, which I hoped would introduce a more lively phase in his behaviour, he became even more retiring. With Freckles gone it seemed that only the buck and doe were coming to the garden. During the next four weeks I found slots of one or the other on most days, for I usually walked round in the early morning looking for traces of overnight activity. The deer were coming into the territory at some time during the night, but the food, except on two occasions, was untouched, though through early summer they had come regularly when herbage was more lush and plentiful.

I made visits to neighbouring woods hoping to encounter the deer, and came across slots which may have been those of the buck and doe. But no white target went up ahead, no clip of flying hoofs disturbed the silence, though I felt that I was probably being watched from the tangled undergrowth. Slots led into an over-grown bramble thicket which I knew the deer inhabited at times, but it was too thick to penetrate even if I had been prepared to risk disturbance, and here I concluded they might be harbouring. In the past, October had usually been a slack month for observation of the deer, and little of the food I put out was taken.

But during the quiet period I continued to find slots in the garden, showing that the territory was being kept under surveillance during the night.

Autumn was for me a time of patient waiting for the deer's return, which usually occurred in early November. But during the last week of October I began to see more slots than usual, and among them those of a smaller deer.

Then came the first frost—a morning clear and brilliant; the birds singing early; the sky swept clean by the tide of a north wind, and regal as autumn, a young buck, slim and golden, antlers almost hidden in the mossy fur of the pedicles—an Adonis among deer.

# CHAPTER 11

# Season of Snow

THE history of Adonis was obscure, but he was accepted by the original buck and doe apparently without question when they returned to the feeding ground a week later, in early November.

I had not encountered buck or doe since late summer, though I often came across their slots in the garden. Their return was heralded by periods of barking; one voice sounding deeper than the other, and in the following week the buck became excited and amorous, grooming and chasing the doe. I heard again the squeaking calls as she ran off with the buck in pursuit, and this with further barking during the week, seemed likely evidence of a rut in progress after the birth of a fawn, though only seven months had elapsed since the birth of Freckles. But the significance of this behaviour was apparent when, about two weeks later, on 23 November, the doe brought a new fawn to the feeding ground. I concluded a rut had taken place, as suspected, after its birth in early November. This also confirmed my suspicions that the sounds of a small animal taking off as I passed a group of bushes about a week ago, had been made by the fawn fleeing from cover, though I had not then seen it. Now it appeared to be from two to three weeks old.

Snow came in December but in no way damped the spirits of the new fawn. For me it brought reflected light with increased detail, and against the simple white background the deer were an inspiration to the animal painter. I thought how well my father, with his fine draughtsmanship and perfection of form, would have rendered the subject.

Travelling over the snow could not have been easy for the deer, but they made their way stoically to the food—Adonis up to his knees, and the fawn to her belly. They stood placidly chewing, and the food was to them a windfall when their natural supplies were snow covered. To lend further charm, the moon, in its first quarter, shone across the garden casting shadows over the unbroken snow, and lighting many places normally too dark to reveal their secrets.

When snow was falling the food soon became covered, but I put a layer of hay over it to keep it dry, and the deer scraped this aside and were able to take the food more or less free from snow.

They had no interest in the hay, though in such cold weather, one felt that they might be expected to eat some to supplement their diet. Only on two occasions have I seen a fawn take a few dry leaves from among the hay, otherwise it has been entirely unacceptable.

At this time, mid-December, the buck began to resent the company of Adonis. When he came to feed he lowered his head towards him, and the young buck walked away, but only to make a detour round the yew, and approach from the other side. He was then sometimes accepted, and the two fed amicably side by side, though when they left, Adonis was always ahead, glancing anxiously over his shoulder at the buck, who followed at a short but purposeful distance.

In the past autumn a friend had undertaken the back-breaking task of collecting acorns, and arrived with a very welcome addition to my store of deer food. These were greatly enjoyed, especially by the fawn, whose skill in dividing the outer shuck from the fruit was fascinating to watch. When she could find no more, she went carefully round the feeding area, nose down, taking any crumbs left by the adults; those of conkers were also sought as she found the unbroken ones hard to dissect.

Many of the deer's feeding habits were repeated as in previous winters, though before, the meals had been taken in complete harmony and now the buck persisted in his resentment towards Adonis. But the young buck had a resilient personality and mild threats did not keep him from feeding. When antlers threatened, he sank low and ran off close to the ground, submissive, but only to retire and stand watching while the buck fed; content to wait his turn.

Though we had passed the shortest day, dusk was still early, and the deer usually arrived at about four-thirty, as the long-tailed tits were congregating on the wire basket of dripping for their last feed before flying away to roost. We had about a dozen coming for fat this winter, and they generally fed several at a time through the day; the entire flock coming together shortly before dusk. I have written in another book of the charm of these tiny birds, and their tameness in coming to feed from the hand; perching freely on one's head or shoulder without any signs of timidity. We lost most of our tame flock in the bad winter of 1962–1963, but they have since made up their losses.

In January the deer came often in daylight, and the pheasants were soon involved with the fawn, as they had been with others in the past. Generally the play took a similar course, but one morning I watched a graceful and airy performance with the fawn leaping towards the pheasant who repeatedly rose on the wing to alight ahead of her, deftly avoiding the nimble little hoofs by her well timed manoeuvres.

When the pheasants were absent the fawn looked for other company, and amused herself by chasing blackbirds on the lawn, running after each in turn till it finally took wing.

For years we have had a considerable pheasant population varying in number from about ten to sixteen, and their liking for garden territory helps to preserve them, though a well known member of the troop disappears from time to time. This was the fate of a handsome melanistic cock whose plumage was exceptionally rich in colour. He haunted the garden for nearly two years but was lost during a shooting season. It was unfortunate that he and the dark hen which arrived later did not come together. She was I think more attractive than the usual breed, and her dark plumage, in which the feathers were edged with lighter colour, had the effect of being laced with gold. But her beauty proved a disadvantage, as the ring-necked cock took exception to her unusual appearance and chivvied her unmercifully in the breeding season. Having called the rest of his harem to the food, he turned to the dark hen keeping her from it with threatening beak, and chasing her across the lawns, through shrubberies and flower borders with fierce determination. At length his persecution became so ruthless that she took wing, settling high in a tree, where she remained preening and waiting patiently till all had finished feeding. Only then was it safe to come down. With several other hens, she became very tame, though unlike one of the paler birds, she never ventured to take food from my hand.

It is significant that the cock tolerated her at other times, and trouble arose only in the breeding season. It seemed that the colour bar in this case was nature's method of keeping the strain pure. I would like to collect evidence to show whether a similar bar actuates in the case of albino birds and mammals. A partial albino blackbird feeds in the sanctuary but unfortunately has not so far bred here, and I have no proof that several juveniles speckled with white, which appeared after the nesting season, were his young, though albinism is said to be hereditary. A white badger cub I watched last year seemed to have no colour problems, though I have yet to see what will happen when she becomes mature.

I have digressed a long way from the present chapter of events among the deer. More snow came in January, and when the fall ceased, I went out with a generous supply of apples and other food, knowing that the deer would come early.

Snow is rarely welcome but its charm is undeniable. The sky had cleared and the setting sun was casting a warm light over the garden; to the east the moon was rising, clear and brilliant with the promise of further frost. Somewhere the deer were harbouring, having found perhaps places under the bushes where less snow had penetrated. I hoped that the fawn I had put up from under a holly hedge in the afternoon had found cover elsewhere. Any protection is doubtless welcome when the ground is an icy couch and snow is drifting. It was a time when the bracken shelters I had made were welcome. It seemed unlikely that the deer could remain inactive for long in such weather without being chilled.

The next day the doe was seen wandering in the garden near to the studio windows, where she came to feed on bramble leaves in the hedge. I saw the deer by daylight more often during the snow, probably because the cold made them restless. It was helpful to be able to sketch without directing torchlight on my book, though I had recently made a sketching block with a covered compartment alongside to hold a torch. This gave sufficient light on the paper without showing the watcher to the deer outside. Adonis especially was very quick to see any movement behind the windows.

Four deer were now coming and as I watched, my thoughts drifted back to the others of the family; the several fawns whose disappearance at varying ages had not been accounted for. I was unaware of surprises to come.

Snowfall had made the deer's movements clearer. I found highways of slots varying in size, and wondered whether we had an additional population as I could not recognise all the tracks. Paths showed where the deer came in and out through the boundaries, and I was glad to see that few slots led across the road where the snow had become hard-packed and slippery from passing traffic.

The deer were hungry and came often, staying to feed for long periods, and one night I glimpsed a small stranger standing in the snow. When later she came near to the house, I was almost certain this was Freckles, the fawn whose birth had been recorded on 30 March of the previous year. I had not seen her since late summer, and she would now be nine-and-a-half months old, an age which appeared to fit this new arrival. The doe fondled and groomed her as her offspring, and why she had been away, or at least invisible for so long, was an unsolved mystery.

The following evening, stepping shyly upon the scene, came a new doe—elegantly poised, in coat of velvet; ears deeply fluted; a ruffle of white fur down her graceful neck—all characteristic of Tiny, last seen in the spring of 1967 when she was about fifteen months old, and who would now be a little over two years. Taller and bigger than the original doe, she was apparently in fawn. It would be interesting to see whether the older doe would tolerate her presence.

The bitter weather continued and icy winds carried the almost continuous calls of hungry fieldfares. A small flock had come in from open country to feed on crabs which still clung to the bough, or were uncovered on the ground by the deer's frequent use of a path they had made below the tree. It formed a highway leading from a thick laurel hedge, a favourite sanctuary for the deer. Apples had been in such short supply that I had harvested some of the crabs in autumn, as they usually rot if allowed to remain on the ground. Few creatures eat these until the worst weather drives them to such unpalatable fare. I scattered some on the lawn near the house, which had the desired effect of bringing the field-fares into closer view. Starlings and blackbirds also feasted on them; an acrid meal, yet taken with relish, particularly if the crabs were broken. Their hardness was a drawback as the birds seemed unable to make a start on any that were not partly rotted. Their efforts sent the crabs rolling across the frozen ground, and some birds gave up the attempt.

Rain and slush that came with the thaw seemed to inconvenience the deer more than snow, and they often appeared uncomfortably wet. But they had a very efficient method of shaking. In a rapid flicker of all muscles from head to tail the water was flung off the

coat as effectively as from clothes in a spin dryer, and the whole process was over in a few seconds.

I saw a lot of grooming between the deer that winter. It appeared to be enjoyed by the fawn, who stood with head stretched out towards the doe, apparently happy to stand for any length of time if she would have continued. The doe took up a similar position when inviting the buck to groom her head and neck, and the two sometimes stood together for a long time, the buck's tongue incessantly smoothing and carressing. When he stopped she thrust her head towards him again, and he obligingly complied.

Grooming, one for another occurs not only among the ungulates, and is shown at its best and most communal in the badger. As many as half-a-dozen of a colony will sometimes spend a long time, on emerging from the sett, close together each grooming the one nearest and receiving the same attentions in return. Grooming is one of the most entertaining features of badger watching, and I have often been tempted to laugh out loud at some of the antics indulged in by a scratching badger. A favourite position, one which I saw taken up by both sow and boar on either side of a sett entrance recently, is that of sitting up on the posterior to comb the soft fur of the belly. This is done by drawing the long front claws through it, sometimes slowly and deliberately, some-

times with a rapid side to side motion; the entire performance appearing to give great satisfaction. Places difficult to reach involve almost acrobatic feats, when a scratching badger may overbalance and roll down the nearest sett entrance, or find himself at the foot of a slope with the cubs romping over him.

With improved lighting for deer observation, I was now able to see them over a wider area, and often watched their more dignified grooming as they drifted about in twos and threes. They were attracted to the old alpine garden where they did little damage as the plants were mostly deciduous. They made many paths throughout the garden though few interfered with plants as they chose the least interrupted ways. But where they walked frequently, the ground was churned up in wet weather, and the grass on the feeding area had to be resown each spring. They were familiar with the shape of every bush, and every shadow there, and learned to expect most of the sounds that issued from the house, though they never became entirely used to the telephone bell. They at once noticed any strange sound or difference in the landscape, and were obviously put out by the fountain of water that suddenly cascaded from a burst stopcock by the pergola during a rapid thaw—a disconcerting sight and sound in the dead of night. I watched the reactions of the doe and Adonis, who had come to feed. Adonis was off at once, but the doe stood her ground for a while, having taken refuge under the yew, wondering perhaps if she could safely regard this as a natural phenomenon. She finally gained sufficient confidence to come out of hiding and investigate, but her courage failed at the last minute, and she withdrew looking anxious and puzzled.

One could watch deer for a lifetime and never know all their ways and individual habits. I had not seen before some aspects of behaviour displayed by the new doe, whose claims to be identified with Tiny, born in December 1965, seemed to entitle her to the use of the name. She had a curious way of stamping a foot repeatedly as she stood listening when suspicious, and one night showed other unusual behaviour. As she strolled on the lawn with the buck, I saw her drop suddenly to the ground and remain there, her head down on the grass, level with her body. The fawn then came into view and running to her, nuzzled her face. After a minute or two Tiny got to her feet, with the fawn prancing happily around her, but she still seemed in a humble mood, and crouching low came up the walk. The fawn followed in high spirits, eventually leaping over her head and then tried persistently to suckle as though she expected all does to be as obliging as her mother.

The submissive action of dropping to the ground was shown again by Tiny that evening, this time at the approach of Freckles. When she came up to the doe they touched noses and Tiny, still lying down, lifted her head and continued to feed, taking any apple within reach. This behaviour occurred several times in the future when other deer joined her by the food.

In late January the original doe began to display unfriendly feeling towards Tiny. At first it was no more than a lowering of head to head, but the younger doe up-tailed, and ran from her, squeaking. Resentment at the other doe's presence was not surprising as Tiny had entered her territory apparently uninvited.

The relationship between Adonis and the fawn was happy, and they frequently came to feed together, running to each other in greeting. Tiny and Freckles seemed to strike up a friendship and were often in company. They went nightly to the shelter under the birches, and could sometimes be seen sharing it; wandering in and out before going on their way. Tiny was also on affectionate terms with Adonis who was willing to groom her head for as long as she desired.

There was plenty to see in the evenings with six deer in the garden, for the buck, though still persistent in his animosity towards Adonis had not succeeded in driving him away. How much the doe was resenting Tiny's presence was difficult to tell, as observation depended on seeing the two together, and Tiny seemed to be keeping out of her way. But one evening when the doe was feeding I saw Tiny approach to stand at a distance while they stared for some minutes at one another. Tiny then diplomatically drifted away. When the doe had finished feeding, she wandered down the walk to the hidden path the younger doe had taken—there was a sudden flash of movement and the two came out across the lawn with the speed of light! They were travelling so fast that I could not see which was ahead, and could only guess that it was Tiny who was being seen off. But she was soon back; though keeping an anxious eye on the surroundings, lest the doe should reappear. Suddenly she lowered her head and froze, listening and watching, and in a minute or so Freckles emerged and came to feed. Tiny apparently failed to recognise her till she was very close, and dropped to the ground as I had seen her do before.

In the February rain, which was often heavy, the feeding ground was reduced almost to a quagmire, and I put down a carpet of hay in an attempt to keep the food clean. There was so much coming and going that the paths leading there became heavily slotted, and any flower borders that were crossed on the way also

suffered from frequent trampling. But this was a small price to pay for the company of deer.

The water garden was one of their favourite haunts, and it was here in mid-February that a deer leapt ahead of me from the bank of the iris pool. He ran up the slope above and stood among the hawthorns for a while before going into deeper cover, and I was able to see that he was a stranger; a young buck with pedicles growing. Presently the original buck wandered from the thicket, apparently tolerant of his presence.

In the evening the visitor came to feed in company with Adonis. They contrasted clearly in pelage and form. The new fawn was a lanky little being, longer on the leg than Adonis, and though younger—his pedicles were little over half-an-inch in length— promised to be of larger type. But the most obvious difference was in colour: he was much darker than Adonis. The pelage was mainly deep umber, mingled with some gold on the face, and the forehead dark brown with facial ribs defined by intense black. As in Adonis, the comparatively lighter underside of the body had the white markings more usually seen in the muntjac doe.

Darky, as he was soon called, seemed not to be of the garden family. No previous fawn corresponded with his estimated age. He and Adonis were as different in temperament as in appearance.

Adonis, calm and self-possessed, the new young buck quick and furtive, always on the defensive, tilting his head at the others as though about to attack; a habit that left Adonis entirely un-ruffled. Perhaps as a stranger in the camp, Darkey never felt com-pletely at ease with the family at that time, though so far none had shown any animosity towards him.

He soon began to show individual traits, the most interesting of which was the setting of scent on the food. Often while feeding or after, he lowered his head and swept it across the remaining food. He continued to act in this way on and off over a long period, and one night by chance I was able to see the opening of the scent glands on the forehead. Normally muntjac use the glands (two frontal, between the facial ribs; two sub-orbital, below the eyes) to anoint saplings beside their paths, presumably to attract the does, and to mark out their territory. This application at the feeding ground seemed a curious one, designed perhaps to lay claim to any food left over. I wondered if he could be induced to set scent in the more usual way, and put up a small sapling by the food, but to my disappointment he ignored it, though several of the deer showed enough interest to sniff the bark.

About this time, hoping to do some sketching of deer browsing on foliage, I pushed some boughs of ivy into the bank beside the feeding ground. These proved very popular. The young deer in particular relished the leaves, perhaps normally above their reach in the hedges, and they were often taken by the fawn in daylight

when no other food was there.

In February the adult buck began to come less, and late in the month disappeared entirely; even his slots were missing from the garden. I thought at first that he may have decided to spend a while away from the family, but this seemed an unlikely time of year for him to leave the food supply, and we had not been without him before in winter. It was sad to see the family incomplete, and Darky's manners might have been improved by some fatherly displine. He was a nuisance to the doe, and sometimes to others by his persistent habit of scenting, and on one occasion I saw the original doe adopt the flat submissive posture before him, though I had never seen her do this throughout the several years she had been here. Running low to the ground in a detour round him was another nervous gesture he provoked. He had too an irritating habit of poking the fawn in the side with his nose; one to which she objected strongly.

Early in March Adonis decided to take him in hand. Watching them from my bedroom at about 2 a.m. I saw him putting on a masterly attitude. He sent Darky from the food, chasing him off so effectively that he dare not stay, as he often did, watching Adonis while he fed. This was followed two nights later by persistent chivvying, with the two running in and out of the bushes; through the alpine garden; back to the food, and off again. Adonis gave the young buck no peace, and with head held high and tail erect came stalking up the grass walk after him, I heard then the castanet call noted before from running deer, and which, seemed, in this instance at least, to be voicing anger.

6 March was a wild night with a sudden snowstorm. Big flakes, catching the light, were whirled in clouds, sweeping towards the ground then spiralling skywards in blizzard frenzy. The fawn arrived with snow flecking her coat, recalling the dappled charm of early days; her spots were now diminishing though a few were to remain visible even to the age of six months.

In spite of the rough night, Adonis was in great form, though it took him nearly a quarter-of-an-hour to drive Darky from the food. He finally took cover while Adonis fed, and when he had finished crept out humbly for his share. After this rout of his dignity I rarely saw them together, and Darky renewed his efforts to make friends with the fawn. He was now growing antlers, which at present appeared as small grey domes. From my records of antler developed in muntjac, I concluded it would be about three months before his antlers were clean and shining, as those that adorned the pedicles of Adonis.

# CHAPTER 12

# Return to Spring

DURING March the deer were often active in the early morning which was ideal for observation and the making of colour notes. But they came also soon after sundown, and I was able to see them at intervals through the night. Unless sleep overtook me, I watched too in the early hours by moonlight, which failed only as the mistle-thrush, from his perch in the larches, signalled the moment of daybreak.

On a warm morning towards the end of the month the chiffchaff was in song: spring had returned, and for several days clear sunshine with temperatures above normal prevailed. But April came in with a sudden change to high gusty winds and shivering conditions of snow and frost. This was hungry weather, and one night the thud of a heavy body on the bird tray brought me to my bedroom window where I met the gaze of a tawny owl, staring back from his perch on the wisteria a few feet away. I supposed that the nimble figure of *Apodemus* had attracted his murderous intentions. The deer too were hungry and took all the food I put out, including some of the wild crabs. At this time the travelling greengrocer, who drives his "shop" to outlying districts, as did the tradesman his horse-drawn wagon years ago, brought some rough apples, sortings from the wholesaler's stock. These were indeed helpful, as my store was nearly exhausted. He also brought a basket of bananas which, apart from blackened skins, were in good condition. I cut some into slices and put them out for the deer, with apples and pears, yet in spite of the cold weather all but the apples were ignored. I continued to offer the bananas nightly as long as they lasted, but every morning found them untouched. To the birds they were a rare luxury, and the pheasants developed a keen appetite for them, which doubtless caused some disappointment when no more were forthcoming.

By mid-April the deer were in summer pelage. The fawn's coat was lighter and more sleek in texture, but it was Darky who showed the most definite change. His pelage was now a bright

Doe—Summer

foxy brown, not many tones darker than the coat of the fair Adonis. The doe showed her usual transformation, having exchanged the dusky tones of winter for summer's chestnut brown.

On 15 April, Tiny, whom I had not seen for a short time, reappeared, slim and elegant and I knew she had dropped her fawn. That night and on the following night I was awakened by deer barking, in the direction of the orchard. The calls were characteristic of rutting; growing fainter then loud and close, with the deer in nuptial chase. From past records it seemed likely that a rut was

Doe—Winter

again taking place following the birth of the fawn. The next evening Tiny came to feed accompanied by Adonis, whose persistent attentions suggested they were paired. Similar behaviour was seen over several evenings with much scenting and chasing by Adonis; Tiny giving shrill squeaks as she ran ahead. After a few nights I saw no more of their amorous association, and they began to come for food separately.

Tiny now seemed to be tolerated by the original doe, for they appeared indifferent to one another. No expressions of resentment, which had occurred earlier, were seen.

Among the flowering shrubs the deer played a decorative part in the garden's spring display. *Magnolia Soulangiana* was in full bloom, a magnificent tree dominating the lawn near the birds' pool, a scene in which the deer were often involved, and as the first blossoms began to fade and fall, the petals were once more a choice item on the menu. On the opposite side of the walk a fine single rose, a rugosa hybrid, had blossomed for years, and its big saucer-shaped petals, flesh pink and white, fell as a delicacy for passing deer. After years of prolific blooming it succumbed, apparently to age, and when its leaf buds failed to break, the bush was cut down and the old twisted stub uprooted. Adonis stood contemplating the empty space, then advanced cautiously to sniff the herbage beneath; puzzled by the changed aspect, for he missed nothing that altered the accustomed landscape.

Life among the deer had reached a quiet period. They came less for food, but one or two usually sauntered up looking for delicacies shortly before dusk. The original doe, now showing signs of being in fawn, often strolled on the walk alone, unconcerned with the affairs of others. She fed for a while then stood listening to the night sounds, sometimes in contemplation of a hedgehog or the bank-voles, who now seemed to have replaced the dashing *Apodemus* in search of peanuts. The voles were more plentiful than usual as seed of a species of scilla, which in the past few years had become invasive, attracted an increased population. This was unwelcome to the gardener, for the tastes of *Clethrionomys glareolus* and *Microtus agrestis* aspire to a variety of choice plants. They always give some trouble in the garden, and bank voles find ample cover under the ferns, from where they run out to eat surrounding herbage. This year scarcely a flowering spike remained on the bluebells over a large area. Hoping for recompense,

# Return to Spring

I went out to a wood where a sea of blossom yearly covers several acres. I found the plants limp and flattened—the Forestry Commission had recently sprayed the entire area in an attempt to rid the wood of brambles which had encroached during the previous year.

The deer's behaviour at this time was uneventful, though Dapple, the fawn of last November, now about six months old, often enlivened the scene. Some interesting examples of relationship between her and the doe evolved. But their meaning was often cryptic, partly because the deer's actions were inconsistent, and the change of mood rapid. I watched the original doe, quietly wandering on the lawn; joined by Dapple, she at once flattened herself on the ground. This I had always taken to be submissive, but when she got to her feet, she turned on the fawn and butted her sharply in the side. Dapple leapt away, but the doe repeated her action following the fawn several times to do so. This appeared to be aggressive, perhaps because the birth of a new fawn was not far away, but Dapple was unperturbed, and in a moment they were in play together butting head-on in light hearted combat. On another occasion I saw the fawn leaping up to the doe repeatedly, trying to induce her to play, and the affectionate grooming which continued from time to time suggested they were on the best of terms.

Darky, who was much too ardent a follower, sometimes prevented the fawn from having her share of the food as he was constantly chasing her. They often arrived together and were seen to touch noses as they met, but whether she enjoyed his company was doubtful. As soon as she began to feed he tried to scent her, and away she went, with Darky in excited pursuit. The relationship of the two young bucks was still far from friendly. Sometimes they fed a yard or two apart, but more often Adonis asserted himself, displaying a threatening attitude that sent Darky running off into cover. But occasionally, though his antlers were not yet hardened, he defied Adonis and was involved in a mild butting dispute. Once, in still bolder mood, I saw him advance, jerking his head up and snapping at Adonis as he came alongside. But he was ignored, and wandered away, tossing his head angrily as he went.

It was certain that Adonis ruled the roost, at least among the younger deer, and the fawn was often at the head of a chase across the garden which involved all three. They emerged from the shrub border to streak over the grass; the fawn leading; Darky, the amorous follower, close behind, and Adonis in turn stalking after him.

With May and the promise of warmer weather very close I was anxious lest the deer stopped coming for food, and Darky, whose antler development I was keen to record, would disappear. But the velvet was already shrinking, and it seemed possible he might stay till his antlers were clean and polished. He maintained his habit of setting scent on the food, though after a while he became less demonstrative in other ways and the fawn had a more peaceful time. Adonis was assuming a more mature form and manner, strutting a little as he walked, dominant in his territory. I noticed too that his tusks (the extended canines in the upper jaw) were

Adonis showing canine

now fully grown and could be seen clearly, though Darky's were not yet visible. When Tiny's fawn came, as it were, into the picture, there would be four different ages for comparison, and perhaps later even five, as the original doe was expecting a fawn. There should be only a month or two between the birth of this one and Tiny's offspring.

I had not yet seen Tiny's fawn, and could scarcely hope to do so till early May. It was in fact the seventh of the month when she made her first appearance, scampering around the doe while she fed. I did not see her again for a time, and found no small slots; she was so light that the finding of tracks depended on her running over suitable ground. Difficulties were increased by a spell of almost continuous rain which frequently obliterated all slots before morning. The place where the deer fed on the grass walk was saturated—so wet that the swallows, who had recently returned to their old nesting site in the tool shed, came down to the bare patch to collect mud for their nest. They had arrived unobtrusively one morning in late April when I was erecting a nesting shelf in anticipation of their coming, and they spent much of the morning flying into and around the shed, twittering joyously as they rested on the short length of cable I had put up for them near the site.

But their contentment was interrupted when, a few days after their arrival, an invading pair suddenly dropped from the sky to compete for the nesting site. There was tremendous activity with the rightful owners chasing the others relentlessly; following in line as they swept over the shed; wheeling across the sky in wide curving flight, to return, diving at breath-taking speed through the gap, little more than a foot wide, between the rain-water pipe and the shed wall. They swept on through the open door in a right-angled turn, and were out again in seconds; the chase halting only when two hung momentarily on the air, hovering beak to beak in shrill chattering dispute.

These arguments continued over the next two days, with the invaders suddenly sweeping in at intervals to renew their attempts to stake a claim on the site. At last peace returned, though the swallows took the easy course of patching last year's nest, ignoring the splendid new shelf, and the container of clay and water supplied for their requirements, and used in previous years.

Their young hatched, and were fledged by the second of July in some of the hottest weather known for years. Close under the shed roof, the nestlings had spent several exhausting days panting from the heat, and I was forced to climb on to the roof at frequent intervals to spray water on the boards and sacking I had put above the nest in an attempt to keep the site cool. Apart from this and the return of the intruders when they were nearly fledged, their nesting days were uneventful. The invading swallows were apparently hoping to build on the shelf I had erected beside the old nest, but were again given short shrift by the nesting pair, and departed after an hour or so of vociferous argument and chasing.

One of the most beautiful events in nature is the first flight of young birds, and with swallows one has the opportunity of seeing this more often than with most species. The birds and young are accustomed to human presence, and in this case were very trusting. Though at first shy, they were soon used to our going into the shed for tools, and the young accepted us as part of the landscape. When at last they took to the air, one after another, to fly accompanied by their parents, it was to try out their wings and settle in surrounding trees. But in a short time they were in their element twisting, turning, arrowing across the sky; a little slower than the adults but scarcely less agile. The first day they quickly disappeared and did not return till about six in the evening. Where they had been and whether they had spent most of the time on the wing was one of nature's mysteries. They seemed glad of the comfort afforded by the shed, and settled down, one on the ledge, the others neatly ranged in the nest. The following morning they were away by half-past-eight and home again by half-past-four in the afternoon, when, strangely, they had collected an additional young bird, near their own age. Five were resting, four perched upright in the nest and the fifth on the shelf beside it. By half-past-nine all were asleep.

The spotted-flycatchers also were fledged that week; the chiffchaffs too were on the wing—a late family following the destruction of the earlier nest by the robber magpie—and five broods of tits had left the nesting boxes in the sanctuary. It was a busy time for the watcher: birds by day, and by night, deer, whose activity I was determined to record more fully than in previous summers. But I had set myself a difficult task; one that was to entail many late and disturbed nights to come.

# CHAPTER 13

# A Fawn in May

IT was over a week since I had encountered Tiny with her fawn, though I had since seen her on a few occasions alone. The last time, one of her eyes was watering profusely, and she appeared to be in great discomfort, as she was unable to keep it open for any length of time and continually soothed it with her tongue. I had seen her, and the original doe affected in this way before. The chance of whipping an eye on the twigs when plunging through a hedge at night must be a frequent hazard. When I did not see her again for a while, I wondered if all was well, for I found neither her slots nor those of the fawn. I was soon to know the reason.

As I watched Adonis and the original doe feeding, they suddenly lifted their heads to stare across the garden as though listening to the approach of another deer. They watched intently for some minutes, then the doe moved quickly forward with head lowered, and at that moment I saw Tiny coming along the path to meet her. There was a frantic squeal, and in the scuffle that followed I caught a glimpse of Tiny extricating herself from the bushes—then tail up! hoofs flying! she was gone! The doe raced after her, and they were at once lost to view. Adonis followed at a more leisurely pace.

This unfriendly reception, and almost certainly others, were doubtless the cause of Tiny's few appearances recently. She and the fawn, if it had been with her, were, I thought, unlikely to return that night. But less than an hour later Tiny sauntered up the walk, followed by the diminutive fawn, indifferent to any arguments that might arise between rival does. This time there were no interruptions and Tiny fed in peace. She showed no anxiety when the fawn went off to explore the surroundings; inquisitive, venturesome, but soon returning to seek assurance that she was not deserted. To emulate the deer's feeding habits seemed instinctive, but a piece of apple was sampled and soon discarded, as were the leaves of hogweed which proved too tough for her milk teeth. The gaiety of her mood was tempered by caution: the sudden barking of a neighbour's dogs sent her running in panic

to the doe, and she froze instantly in what may have been her first encounter with a field-mouse. But doubts soon passed, and snipping off a daisy head, she was away again, her foxy brown pelage, speckled with large though indistinct spots, glimpsed here and there among the ferns.

After a few nights Tiny came again, and while she fed, the fawn wandered up the bank almost to the windows, then with sudden impulse returned to rub her slim little head against the doe's face; a gesture I often saw exchanged between them. The fawn drifted about the feeding ground, sniffing the food, though she took very little and was at this age dependent mostly on the mother's milk. But Tiny was not always willing to let her suckle when she was feeding herself, and the fawn's minute tongue moved rapidly in and out in vain at the prospect.

It was disappointing when after a while they failed to come, and I found few slots on their accustomed paths. The possibility that the fawn had been killed by a roving fox or dog could not be discredited, but I knew from past happenings that all might still be well, and they would be encountered again, perhaps the next night, or in a week, or a month hence.

The other deer were still seen and were abroad early in the evenings, so early that they were lucky to find any food, with birds and squirrels constantly searching for more. We had at that time a renegade magpie in the garden—a veritable pirate. He had arrived in the previous spring, limping slightly and with one wing drooped, a handicap which probably accounted for his coming to feed with the small birds near the house. As he matured he became an inveterate egg thief. His spoils were found scattered across the lawn:

the remains of eggs stolen from the nests of song-thrushes, black-birds, starlings, tree-sparrows and wood pigeons. Doubtless many others suffered his depredations. One day, hearing the chiffchaffs weeping, I caught the villain in the act. But I was too late, the feathered lining of the nest littered the ground—the eggs were gone. In the evening he had the audacity to come to feed beside the deer, regarding Darky with tilted head and watchful eye, but venturing close enough to snatch peanuts. These he carried down the garden, and later collected into a cache covered with moss, where I found them next morning.

The following evening, the pirate, fancying a more substantial meal, attacked *Apodemus* when he came out for his share. But the mouse was too quick for him; though he waited, for some time, still as a cat, peering under the fern where the mouse had retreated, it was too wary to show itself again.

The magpie treated the deer with caution, but not with the respect he showed for the grey squirrels. The male, always posses-sive, sat squarely over the food, while the bird sidled up half afraid, stabbing ineffectively with his beak, for the squirrel con-tinued to eat as though nothing untoward was happening.

Eventually the magpie met his match in his own reflection. Our nextdoor neighbour, awakened at dawn by a fearful clatter downstairs, crept out of bed to rout the supposed intruder, and making a stealthy approach, peered down from the landing to see a big bird—the same magpie—battering himself repeatedly against the French windows. Leaping high in the air with wings outspread he put tremendous vigour into the assault, determined to oust what he presumed to be another cock in his territory. These uneven contests, which mostly occurred soon after daybreak, were repeated over a period of about four weeks, with assaults frequent during the first ten days, and decreasing through the rest of the time. They were watched occasionally by his mate, perched on a low garden wall behind him, apparently unmoved.

Instances of birds attacking their own reflections are not un-common, though they are usually seen as the action of small birds. There are fewer reports of the bigger birds performing in this way, perhaps because they are less often associated with houses. Though windows are frequently involved, there have been similar inci-dents with car headlamps and other bright surfaces which reflect as mirrors.

# Muntjac

With the coming of the long light evenings, in which the deer were liable to appear at any time from eight o'clock onward, the trouble from grey squirrels increased. I had foreseen this earlier in the year when I watched the female carrying her young, one after another, from some distance away to a new nest in a tall Italian poplar bordering the garden. Whether she had made the move through disturbance of the original nursery, I never knew, but I regarded with apprehension the addition to the family, and the difficulties it might entail later.

I heard and saw nothing further of the young squirrels till the end of May when they became a nuisance taking the deer's food, and were so tame that their appearances in the kitchen among the saucepans were a cause of dismay. Every open window was an invitation, and any food put out for birds or deer was instantly pounced upon. The squirrels fought over it, and the biggest of the three, sent the other two squealing from the scene. One could not deny that they were amusing in spite of the annoyance they

caused. They poked their inquisitive noses into everything. A rustle of paper brought me at a run to the box of groceries left on the doorstep, from which I saw a waving tail protruding; the owner, for once caught off guard, was well down into a packet of biscuits!

As the squirrels rarely retired to their drey till about nine p.m. and the doe was coming nightly for food soon after eight, it was difficult to ensure that any remained for her under the heap of grass which covered it, however deeply. The same items of food were put out on the lawn to lure any invaders from the deer's share, but the squirrels in particular were convinced that something more tasty was hidden for the deer. They burrowed down into the heap to reach the food almost within seconds. But this was not enough, when the gooseberries began to form they raided the fruit cage reaching the fruit with their paws through the wire mesh, and in spite of shouts and recriminations, sat on top of the cage devouring the gooseberries rapidly one after another. When all that could be reached from the outside, had been taken, and the raspberry crop was ripening, they gnawed holes in the overhead netting and had a riotous time among the bushes and canes.

There was a more agreeable scene in the wild garden where I found Darky and Adonis browsing together, unaware that they were being watched. They seemed now almost inseparable; a strange relationship, for Adonis continued to bully the younger buck, sometimes allowing him to feed near-by, but more often chasing him from the food. The chivvying continued up and down the banks of the old alpine garden and round the birches till Darky became so exasperated that his temper was roused and he retaliated, snapping, as I had seen him do earlier, when he first joined the deer. Yet the two never came seriously to blows.

Darky, whose antlers had been just visible by 12 March, was now, towards the end of May, still in velvet, though the tips of his antlers were almost clean. About this time his beauty was temporarily marred by a scratch down his nose, and a deeper one across the shoulders. Earlier Dapple had received a similar scar along her side, though it appeared to be only superficial. Later I saw that Adonis too was marked; in his case along the back. The damage was not serious, but it troubled me as it suggested that the deer were going through a barbed-wire fence where, if anything caused them to rush the gap, injury could be severe.

On 26 May I saw that the original doe had resumed her previous shapely figure, and knew that somewhere in the herbage a new fawn was hidden.

With Tiny's Tim—a name that seemed inevitable—we now had two fawns younger than any two which had come together before in the garden. Tim, born in mid-April, was about six weeks old, and the association of the two promised some enjoyable watching. But this could not be expected yet.

The doe was keeping the whereabouts of her fawn a close secret, though she was coming to feed with the other deer in the evenings, and I concluded it was not far away. Anxious to see it I intensified my observation, sometimes watching from the bedroom window through most of the night. I often saw the deer in the early hours, and more than once heard repeated barking which, with the finding of a newly made series of paths around bushes in the wild garden, again suggested a rut following the birth of a fawn.

Though I had no evidence that the doe was driving Dapple away she left at the beginning of June and I wondered if this had any connection with the arrival of the new fawn. I was still seeing all the other deer, including Darky, whose antlers were clean by 9 June—three months from the date of casting, as with the adult buck of the previous year.

When the fawn was about two weeks old I found her tiny slots by the feeding ground, though in spite of disturbed nights I had missed her coming. Several times I saw her tracks there and in other places, though by chance she eluded me for a further week. Then suddenly I was rewarded. She was a slim little figure, for her pelage lacked the full fluffiness generally seen in winter fawns. (A feature I had noted in Tiny's Tim, also born in time of summer pelage.) Sleek and dainty, the smallest of the family, she became identified as Pip. She was well spotted and differed in this respect from previous fawns in having a distinct line of speckles along her neck from shoulder to ear. I wish she had kept her spots longer, but they were to almost disappear by the time she was five weeks old; a normal procedure, except with Dapple, whose spots had remained longer than any.

The two fawns were delightful together and both at the playful age. Tiny's Tim appeared to seek the company of the younger fawn and the doe, who was usually with her. But I felt that the parents were probably not on such good terms. When I saw the does together, which was rarely, Tiny seemed uncertain of her

A Fawn in May

reception, and was soon away. I could not of course tell what
occurred unseen, though one night when the original doe left,
taking the hidden path under the magnolia, there was a sudden
squealing, and Adonis, who was at that time often with Tiny,
emerged alone. It seemed probable that Tiny had once more been
driven off by the jealous doe.

Near the end of June Adonis cast his antlers. His new year had
begun—three months in which to regain his full attire; about nine
months before his antlers were cast again.

This summer I saw more of the deer than I had at that season
in any previous year. A number continued to come throughout the
period, and there was no slackening of their visits till the end of
September. Even Tiny, whom the doe had done her best to banish
from the territory, had not left entirely. But her appearances were
few and she did not, to my knowledge, come after the end of
August. But in early July a small doe, whom I believed to be
Freckles, came upon the scene. She would now be about fifteen
months old, and appeared pregnant, which was possible if she had
mated early. She much resented Pip's desire to suckle, and turned
on her angrily. She did not stay long in the territory, and I never
saw her with the expected fawn.

During August, my assumptions that Tiny's Tim was of the
stronger sex were qualified by his behaviour. The frequent chasing
of the younger fawn, and his persistent desire to scent her and the
doe, were typical of a young buck. He continued, as Darky had
done, to set scent on the food, and on one occasion I saw him
attempt to mount the buck during an interval of play and butting
between them. It seemed that by chance the name bestowed
upon him was of the correct gender.

As he grew, Tim became strongly reminiscent of Darky. He too
was tall, and he had the same lanky raw-boned figure. Back view
there was a great similarity, for his tail, which was a mark of dis-
tinction, was, as in Darky, longer and broader than that of any
of the other deer, except perhaps Tiny. Several of the habits of the
earlier young buck were being repeated by him. The two were in
many ways so alike that I felt Tim must surely be the brother of
Darky, who had appeared mysteriously and whose origin I have
been unable to trace. He had come to the garden about a month
after the doe assumed to be Tiny had returned. Her age would
allow for Darky to have been her first fawn, and Tim, born about

15 April of this year, her second. She had grown into a taller and bigger doe than the original one of the garden, characteristics which were clearly apparent in the two fawns.

As summer progressed the deer began to make surprise appearances by day. The doe was seen wandering on the slopes of the alpine garden, browsing where brambles and a variety of weeds, which we had been unable to keep at bay during the wet summer, were encroaching from the wild garden beyond. Occasionally she lay down beneath the trees, and we were confined to the house while she spent a leisured half-hour or more resting and ruminating. The fawns too had become unusually bold and both came with the doe sometimes long before sunset. But it was Tim who made the most daring venture. We had been standing for some time on the pergola talking to a friend, when I suddenly saw a movement under the golden yew, and Tim, leaving cover, came out on to the grass below the steps, no more than a few paces from where we stood. He stared at us, but did not retreat, and we watched him in silence while he sniffed the ground, looking for food, which had not yet been put out, for he had come an hour earlier than usual. He wandered, appeasing his appetite by snipping off a few leaves here and there, and when he was hidden from view, I tossed out some peanuts from my pocket. Presently he returned and taking another long look at the three people tormented by midges but trying desperately to keep still, he came forward tempted by the nuts. But he was not satisfied, and waited, expectant; standing for a while to chew a mouthful of herbage, or to scratch delicately behind an ear. When he had at last strolled beyond the shrubs, I crept away to fetch some food while the opportunity occurred. But my return was unfortunate, as the doe had joined him meanwhile. They stood together under the birches, and the approach though cautious proved too much for their tolerance—they were away at once! It seemed likely that after this indiscretion on my part they would not return till late, but in half-an-hour they were back and feeding as usual.

The boldness of the deer at this time was mystifying, and I was equally at a loss for an explanation of their behaviour when I awoke one night in the early hours to hear a fawn giving voice. The barks, which were high pitched and resembled the excited yapping of a puppy, were followed by piping calls, shrill and bird-like. Another young voice answered, and both continued to call for some time, with the first fawn's barking and piping calls growing fainter as she ran towards the eastern boundary. The two were, I presumed, Pip and Tiny's Tim. But it was impossible to tell whether the calls were merely an exchange of argument or the result of disturbance, perhaps by a dog or fox ranging the garden. I was apprehensive, but the following evening the two fawns and the other deer were seen, and all appeared to be normal. If there had been any trouble that night none seemed affected. But next morning when Tim came in daylight I saw that the skin had been grazed below his left eye, and could only assume that he had been driven in panic against a fence or similar barrier.

Tim was advanced for his age. He was scarcely five months, though the tufts of pedicle growth were already visible, and his interest in members of the opposite sex had been evident for some time. He wandered with the doe and Pip frequently and appeared to be in fine form. Almost the last I saw of him was in a flying leap that spanned the wide gulley of the alpine garden, when he wanted to join the doe on the other side. After one more night, which began with his usual daylight appearance in the evening, I did

not see him again, and a night when I saw no deer, though I watched till one-thirty a.m. probably held the secret of his disappearance.

Near the end of September the deer became very erratic in their visits, but I was able to see Adonis on and off till his antlers were cleaned; as usual about three months from casting.

The reason for the deer's absence or partial absence from the territory during October—a phase of behaviour repeated yearly—was obscure. Though they visited the garden almost nightly, and ate some of the food put out, I felt they had probably taken up headquarters farther afield. I saw them on few occasions, and found the doe's slots more often than those of the buck and fawn, who usually seemed to be absent. The visits occurred mostly long after midnight, and I never encountered the deer in the early morning. Possibly their new territory was some distance away, and they were leaving early to reach their lairs by dawn. This routine was broken only on rare occasions by the appearance of the doe at about 10 p.m. Once Adonis came in daylight, just before sunset, looking hungry and thin, with ribs showing. The doe and Pip were also in the garden that evening.

After his brief appearance, Adonis departed again, and I wondered if he was away consorting and fighting with other bucks which happened to be in hard horn at that time of year. For this he may have travelled long distances, which would account for his run down condition.

Most of the deer were away this autumn much longer than usual. But the doe continued her nightly visits, and Adonis returned during the last week of November, having apparently regained his full weight and vigour. I then began to see him and the doe every night, and after a while found the tracks of a third deer. On the first of December Tiny came with Adonis in attendance, seemingly much enlivened by her return. Eight months had passed since the the birth of Tim, and the last rut between her and Adonis, and one evening she strolled into the light followed by a small spotted fawn, which appeared to be little more than a week old. Soon after, Adonis, who had been inseparable from Tiny, transferred his affections—the original doe was expecting a new fawn. The full cycle of life among the deer was turning again.

# CHAPTER 14

# Summary

THE previous chapters are a record taken from my diaries of the past eight years. They relate from year to year through the seasons the behaviour and movements of the deer, and the happenings that have occurred among them. This, the last chapter, classifies the knowledge gained, under specific headings which deal in turn with the habitats favoured by muntjac; with the animals themselves, their general physical features; behaviour and temperament; reproduction and development; voice and communication; feeding habits and diet, and finally with their yearly cycle. In this summary the main facts and conclusions can be found together and the whole used in conjunction with the appendix for reference.

## Habitats

Cover is the first requirement of muntjac, and woodland, which often forms much of their environment, must provide plenty of low herbage and thickets of dense undergrowth where the deer can lie up and establish their sanctuaries. Deciduous woods are preferred, as plantations of coniferous trees rarely allow the growth of sufficient low cover. Where established woods have been cut down and young trees planted, the herbage which quickly springs up during reafforestation may provide suitable habitat, giving seclusion and food supply from wild ground cover. But woodland is not the only type of environment favoured. Overgrown wasteland and areas of thick scrub are also acceptable, and muntjac seem attracted to steep undulating terrain. I have found well worn paths on almost perpendicular banks, and where disused gravel pits have become rank with bramble, broom, and gorse any deer in the area soon discover them. Whether the precipitous nature of the land is in itself an attraction or merely incidental to cover, one cannot tell. Certainly there may be added safety in a sanctuary placed on high ground with steep approaches, and the valleys between escarpments give shelter from rough weather. I have noted signs of deer in several such areas. Muntjac are very sure footed and often use paths down slippery inclines though there are alternative routes. In the garden they have no trouble in negotiating stone steps and bridges.

Long established gardens which offer the seclusion of shrubberies are attractive to these small deer, and they will lie up all day if herbage is sufficiently dense. Edible ground cover is much appreciated, and where ivy abounds it is frequently browsed. Paths are made through the herbage, as the deer often walk nightly in the same tracks, and bare places can be seen where they lie down to rest and ruminate. In most of the habitats I have explored, a woodland pool or a pond has been available, though the deer probably obtain enough moisture in their diet, except in dry weather, when I have often seen them drinking in the garden.

Muntjac retire into cover for most of the day, but if undisturbed may come out to browse at any time. Clearings in woodland are likely places for daylight activity, but to see the deer is not easy as the litter underfoot prevents a silent approach. Anyone walking on the dry leaves and twigs of a woodland floor will be heard by the deer long before he is aware of them. By carefully following a deer path (which should not be walked upon) one may come across a clearing with signs of frequent activity. Bramble and other herbage is often browsed around the perimeter, and a lair or two formed under cover at the edge. Sometimes the ground beneath a big tree is heavily slotted on the sheltered side where deer stand out of prevailing wind. If it is possible to reach such a clearing without being heard, and to take cover before the deer arrive, they may be seen there even in daylight, for they enjoy sunning themselves, and must come into the open to do so.

Muntjac tend to inhabit gardens more in winter when they probably wander less, and wilder habitats become exposed and subject to discomfort from cold, and searching winds. Where deer are well established the area is interspersed by paths and runways, whose current use can be determined, when the ground is damp, by the appearance of fresh slots. Along such paths the results of casual browsing are seen; a few shoots of holly, or leaves taken from bramble, ivy and other wild plants. The bark of a sapling may show where the buck has set scent or polished his antlers. Sometimes a few droppings are found, though the deer's main lavatories are

### Summary

usually among shrubs or in thickets.

Almost any cover is acceptable to muntjac, though where ground cover provides food it is doubtless an additional attraction. The dense thorny retreat offered by briar and bramble will probably be preferred to an area of bracken which dogs and foxes can penetrate quickly.

## General Physical Features

The casual observer usually sees muntjac running or leaping away, when identification is difficult to all but the initiated. The back view, when fleeting, can be confused with those of two other species of similar size: native roe deer, *Capreolus capreolus,* and Chinese water-deer *Hydropotes inermis.* But rump patterns and differences in tails are useful guides. In roe the tail is scarcely evident, but in muntjac is about five inches long; in both the white target is prominent. But in Chinese water-deer tail and target are less conspicuous. When tracks are visible the identification of muntjac is made certain by the imprint of unequal cleaves, but unless the slots are clearly defined this point may be missed.

The buck is the easiest to identify, as the facial ridges and long pedicles supporting the antlers are a sure feature of recognition, though the question of whether the deer is Indian, Chinese or a cross still has to be decided. Indian muntjac are of course unlikely to be encountered as none is thought now to be feral in England.

### RUMP PATTERNS

MUNTJAC

Buck                                           Doe

Chinese water-deer                    Roe deer

## RUMP PATTERNS

The differences between *Muntiacus reevesi* and a cross are difficult to determine in the field.

Full descriptions of muntjac pelage will be found in the appendix. When identifying deer allowance should be made for variations in colour of individuals, and for changes to summer and winter pelage. The winter coat is assumed during October, and the return to summer pelage in the following April to May.

The antlers, present only in the buck, are cast annually and the regrowth and hardening takes about three months. In common with other events in the life of muntjac, this occurs at varying seasons according to individuals.

In the buck the canines are developed as curved tusks, about three-quarters-of-an-inch long. These are first visible when the deer is around eighteen months old. They are said to be employed in defence.

Mature buck                          Yearling

## Summary

The scent glands are used by the buck to anoint saplings, with the intention of attracting does in the area, and to mark out territory. Scent is also set on food. The frontal glands are not visible in the field unless being used, but the slits to the sub-orbitals can be seen, and may be open if the deer is frightened or in pain.

It is said that muntjac have poor eyesight, but the slightest movement is detected instantly, and in my experience they appear to see very well. The eyes are typically large and lustrous, and the observer finds it hard to approach at all times without being seen. Hearing is acute and the ears can be turned independently to enable the deer to detect the approach of danger from more than one direction.

The feet of muntjac are peculiar in having uneven cleaves. Differences in the front and back feet are seen in the slim pointed cleaves of the front compared with the shorter and more rounded form of the back. The hoofs, which are small and neat, are often used for scratching the body, and in grooming; a purpose shared with the tongue, which is long enough to enable the deer to reach the eyes.

# Behaviour and Temperament

The extreme shyness of muntjac is frequently demonstrated and dominates their way of life. But over the years I have been watching the deer in the garden they have gradually become less retiring. The chief periods of muntjac activity normally occur at dusk, through the night and in the early morning, and they retire to their sanctuaries or lairs in cover generally between eight-thirty and nine a.m. During the day it is their habit to lie up for several hours, then to emerge and take a little food, returning to the lair to rest and ruminate. A fawn watched in a lair by day was seen to groom her coat frequently and to doze at intervals. She emerged several times to feed and wander a short distance before going back into cover. At dusk she left for more intensive feeding and nightly activity.

Muntjac generally live in small family parties, with the young does tending to drift from home ground from the age of six months and over. Occasionally one may be driven out by the reigning doe shortly before the birth of a new fawn, but I have often seen the previous fawn enjoying immunity and later accompanying the doe and her new fawn. Some remain even to the age of fifteen months. Though usually placid and tolerant, the doe may become aggressive towards any other mature doe in her territory if the birth of her fawn is imminent.

Young bucks are mostly permitted to stay till they are over a year old, when they become competitive to the reigning buck. The length of time they are tolerated varies with their sexual development. Once driven out they are not seen in the territory again, but the young does often return to the parents even after an absence of several months, though the older doe keeps her dominant position in the family.

Play sometimes occurs between young deer, and has been seen on a number of occasions in the garden in daylight. This takes the form of crouching, leaping, butting and rapid chasing of one deer by another. I have not seen play among adults, but mock contests sometimes take place between the buck and a young fawn.

Grooming plays a frequent part in the social life, and is exchanged by deer regardless of sex. Licking of head, neck and shoulders is often continued for a long time. It appears to be an enjoyable pastime for both, and with similar demonstration suggests friendly, if not affectionate, relations among members of a family.

The buck and doe share the same territory through most of the year, and may be seen together at almost any time. The muntjac buck appears usually to be monogamous, though in the garden the present buck has almost certainly mated with a second doe; barking typical of the rut, and the attentions he paid to her around the time of the birth of her fawn, strongly suggested pairing.

The number of deer coming to a feeding ground increases in winter, particularly when the weather is cold and food scarce. I have noticed that the approximate ages and the sex of such deer often correspond with those of fawns of the family which have been missing meanwhile for varying periods. The second doe, mentioned in the previous paragraph, was thought to be a fawn of the reigning doe, returned after maturity.

In temperament muntjac are extremely timid. They frequently stay in cover, taking advantage of low herbage and standing crops, where they are unnoticed. But if allowed to remain undisturbed in a wild garden they become to some extent used to human presence, though the distance they will permit anyone to approach is strictly limited. They usually go into cover at the least hint of danger, but will on occasions stand in the open for some minutes to watch one's movement, and marked boldness is sometimes displayed by young deer.

Though I have seen deer feeding untroubled by almost continuous flashes of lightning, high wind always alarms them; the noise and movement combined makes them very furtive. They do not seem to be much inhibited by moonlight unless it is accompanied by wind, when the moving shadows cause additional disturbance. In heavy rain they seek shelter, but will come out to feed in moderate rainfall.

# Reproduction and Development

Muntjac have no fixed time of year for rutting, and the seasons vary with individuals. Fawns may be born in any month, and mating generally takes place soon after the birth. A single fawn is usual. Twins have not yet been recorded in this country. The period of gestation is approximately from seven to eight-and-a-half months, and the doe is almost continually pregnant. Unless there is a second rut during the eight months or so, and I have no evidence of this, the gestation period seems a long one for such small deer. Though evidence is so far inconclusive, it suggests the possibility of delayed implantation in the breeding cycle, as in roe deer, the badger and a number of other mustelids—a condition in which development of the embryo (at this stage known as the blastocyst) is halted for a time, so lengthening the period of gestation.

Near to the birth of a fawn, the buck begins to show special interest in the doe, and shortly after the birth, periods of barking occur, usually by night and in the early hours. Sometimes it is evident, from the changing volume of the calls, that the deer are on the move, with the buck chasing the doe. In more than one instance following this I have found the area of their activity interlaced by newly made runways encircling bushes and groups of wild herbage where chasing has taken place. Over this period and occasionally before, the buck's attentions to the doe are increased. His desire to scent her is persistent, and she runs off giving a high-pitched squealing call. The buck follows, and barking may then be heard. After about a week he becomes less amorous, but still accompanies the doe. His attachment to her and the family continues through most of the year, though I have rarely seen him with the doe in

October.

During the fawn's first week of life the doe leaves it hidden in the undergrowth, returning at intervals to allow it to suckle, and it probably does not travel far. Those of the garden have come with the doe to the observed feeding ground at ages of about ten days to four weeks. They soon begin to take a small amount of solid food, though they continue to suckle for several months. I have seen attempted suckling by a fawn of six months.

The characteristics of the young buck and doe develop gradually Differences in the shape of the head become apparent around five months old, when the buck begins to show a straighter profile than the young doe as the bone structure of the facial ridges, which will later extend to pedicles, is more strongly developed. Habits of the male, as chasing and scenting other deer, are first displayed at differing ages; some fawns develop more quickly than others. Tufts which are the first indication of growing pedicles, can be seen at from five-and-a-half to seven months. Pedicles and antlers are formed rapidly, though the whole process of growing, hardening, and cleaning takes about three months. Soon after this the buck is presumably mature, and the tusks in the upper jaw are visible. Fifteen months appears to be a likely age for maturity in the muntjac doe.

In the fawns I have studied in the garden the length and fluffiness of the first pelage has varied in individuals. The longer fur seems more often to occur in winter fawns than in those of summer, when the pelage is more sleek. Possibly fawns born during the period when the adult is in summer pelage have summer coats, and the cold weather is provided for by the warmer pelage of winter. But many more records are needed before a definite conclusion can be reached.

# Voice and Communication

The chief call of muntjac is a harsh persistent bark. When alarmed, the deer runs off to stand at a distance, where he may continue barking for half-an-hour or more. The buck and doe bark in communication, and the doe will often call in alarm if she is disturbed with her fawn. In contrast to this loud barking, a scarcely audible sound, resembling muffled castanets, is sometimes emitted by running deer. This is said to be caused by the expulsion of breath. I have heard it on more than one occasion, and when watching a yearling chasing off a younger buck it seemed clearly to be an expression of anger. There is too, the squeaking call of the doe mentioned under *Reproduction and Development*. The voice of the fawn is a shrill version of the adult bark, and is sometimes combined with a clear bird-like or piping call.

# Food and Feeding Habits

Muntjac are fastidious in their choice of food: the deer of the garden have a preference for sweet apples, which in winter are eaten in quantity with conkers, sweet chestnuts, acorns and peanuts. The natural diet in the wild includes grass and other foliage, as buttercup, hogweed, dandelion; also leaves of holly, ivy, bramble and various trees. Fungi is eaten occasionally. Wild rose hips are taken, but I have little evidence of muntjac's liking for berries in general. Blackberries and other wild fruits have not been taken when put out on the observed feeding ground. A list of foods eaten and foods refused can be found in the following appendix.

Feeding is often communal, but the buck will sometimes drive a younger buck from the food when he is becoming mature and shows territorial ambitions. These are opposed by the reigning buck, who chases him away at almost every opportunity, and he must wait his turn to feed when the older buck is absent.

The deer feed from dusk onward through the night and early hours, wandering meanwhile or resting in cover, where they ruminate, and groom their coats. Sometimes in cold weather they feed for half-an-hour at a time, returning at intervals for more. Feeding is mostly by night, though a deer may come out of hiding to take a small amount of food at any time of day. Browsing is generally from ground to head level, though I have seen leaves taken from boughs so high that the deer must have stood on the hind legs to reach them. Browsing is casual; a few leaves taken in passing, which mitigates any damaging effect.

Individual deer show marked preferences for specific food which others refuse or take sparingly, and certain items offered at the feeding ground have no attraction at given times of year. But with the onset of cold weather there is a return to all foods normally taken through winter.

# The Yearly Cycle

This bears little relation to the cycle of our native deer, in whom physiological changes and movements occur at given times of year. For muntjac, events take place at differing seasons: the birth of the fawn, the rutting, and casting of antlers can occur in almost any month, and the times for these happenings in an individual's life are largely governed by the month of the first mating, which begins the sequence of events for the doe. One cannot therefore set down the yearly cycle of muntjac in general, and I will describe, as far as present knowledge allows, the happenings in the cycle of one family, taking as an example a buck and doe who mated soon after the birth of a fawn in late May. The family will remain together for most of the summer, and the buck may cast his antlers a few weeks after the rut. (Whether this is always so I cannot say till a greater number of instances have been recorded.) During the regrowth of the antlers he can still be seen with the doe, and probably does not wander far outside his own territory.

In October the family drifts apart, and the buck in particular is rarely seen on home ground. Fawns who have become independent often vanish about this time or earlier, but the doe seems still to frequent the territory consistently. The buck's visits are few and he may wander several miles to consort with other bucks at this time. During November he rejoins the doe, with whom he associates through the winter, when some of the previous fawns may also return. The doe, mated in May, will have her fawn at some time from the end of December to mid-February, and this event concludes the cycle.

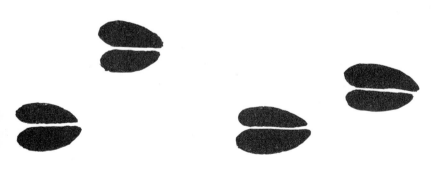

Muntjac slots

# Appendix

## Genus Muntiacus

The following notes, except where otherwise indicated are from my own observations of *Muntiacus spp.* Identification of *M. reevesi* in garden confirmed by comparison of skull with those in British Museum (Natural History) with the assistance of Mr. Robert W. Hayman, Department of Zoology. We could find no evidence to show that my specimen was that of a hybrid.

'A good character separates the skulls of *M. reevesi* and *muntjak* at any age in both sexes.

In *reevesi* the premaxillae do not, at their upper end, make contact with the lateral margins of the nasals, since a narrow extension of the maxilla separates the two.

In *muntjak* the premaxillae make clear contact with the lateral edges of the nasals with no interruption by the maxilla.'

Robert W. Hayman

'Genus has five species, all small animals with simple antlers and tusk-like canines, and all confined to S. and S.E. Asia apart from introductions. Recorded up to 6,500 ft. in Himalayas.

Indian Muntjac (Barking Deer) *Muntiacus muntjak* (Zimm.) Chinese Muntjac *M. reevesi* (Ogilby).

First species has eight subspecies distributed from China through India down to Malaya and E. Indies. Introduced at Woburn 1890. Chinese species has one main form from China and dubious one from Formosa. Introduced at Woburn 1900.'

*The Handbook of British Mammals*

*Muntiacus reevesi* and its hybrid with Indian muntjac have become widely distributed since both species were liberated in the outlying woods around Woburn. By 1964 occasional reports of the deer's appearance had come from at least a dozen counties, and Mr. F. J. Taylor Page recorded the spread of muntjac out from Bedfordshire, north to Derbyshire, east to Norfolk, south to Middlesex, Hampshire and Sussex, south west to Dorset and west to the Cotswolds and into Monmouthshire. He now brings the list up to date by the inclusion of the New Forest, N.E. Sussex, Bushey Park, Richmond Park, Surrey and (unconfirmed) Kent.

# Pelage

BUCK, SUMMER: Chestnut brown on back and sides; deep golden underparts; legs blackish brown; head golden; forehead brown; black facial lines down inner side of pedicles merging into dark grey above nose and converging above forehead; ears dusky with light edges; golden inside; no white except under tail and on target. WINTER—Pelage a little darker.

DOE, SUMMER: Chestnut brown on back and sides; legs blackish brown; head golden; forehead brown, black facial lines merging into dark grey over nose; black converging above forehead; black line over top of head meeting brown of neck; ears dusky with light edges; white to cream inside; white on top lip, chin, under neck, chest, belly, things and tail and on target; tail and around target ginger. WINTER—dark chocolate brown above; otherwise much as in summer.

FAWN, APPROXIMATELY 7½ MONTHS. MALE. NOVEMBER 1965: Dark chocolate brown on back and sides; golden below; legs blackish brown; head golden; forehead rich brown; black facial lines converging across top of forehead; ears dusky, edged light; golden inside; tufts of hair indicating pedicle growth; pelage thick, dense and velvety in appearance, very fluffy under jaws.

FAWN, DARK VARIANT. ABOUT 8 MONTHS. MID-FEBRUARY 1968: Dark foxy umber on back and side; suffused

Appendix

golden below; legs sooty; head suffused golden; forehead dark brown; black facial lines converging above forehead; ears dusky, edged light; light umber inside; white on top lip and chin; white to cream under neck, chest, belly and thighs; white on target and under tail; pedicles about $\frac{1}{2}$ in.

## YOUNG BUCK, PALE VARIANT. LITTLE OVER A YEAR.
EARLY NOVEMBER 1967: Light golden umber back and sides; legs dusky brown; head and forehead golden; jet black facial lines down inner side of pedicles and converging above forehead; ears dusky with light edges, pale golden inside; white on top lip and chin as in adult doe; pale cream under neck, chest and belly, white under tail and on target; pelage sleek; antlers approximately 1 in.

## YOUNG DOE, APPROXIMATELY 18 MONTHS. JANUARY
1966: Dark brown on back and sides, legs sooty; head golden; forehead umber; black facial lines merging to grey above nose; black converging above forehead; black line over top of head to neck; ears dusky edged light, white inside; white on top lip, chin, under neck, chest, belly, thighs and tail, and on target; bright ginger on tail around target and on demarcation line; colour generally brighter and cleaner than in older doe; form slim and youthful; head slim.

### SPOTTED FAWNS

Colour varies with individuals. In some the coat is dark brown with spots not sharply defined; in others golden brown with spots pale cream; white under tail and on target in all variants and at all ages. The spots begin to fade early and by four or five weeks have almost disappeared; the coat gradually becomes less fluffy.

## FAWN, APPROXIMATELY 1-2 WEEKS. JANUARY 1959:
Golden brown pelage paling to cream on underparts; spots pale cream, clearly defined; head golden, forehead brownish, black facial lines converging across top of forehead and line over back of head meeting brown on neck; ears dusky with light edges; cream to white inside; white on chin, under thighs and tail, and on target; pelage fluffy, specially under jaws and down neck.

FAWN, APPROXIMATELY 2–3 WEEKS. FEMALE. DECEM-
BER 1965: Dark chocolate brown on back and sides, paling below,
legs dusky; spots indistinct; head golden; forehead umber; black
facial lines, ears dusky, edged light, pale golden inside; white
under tail and on target. THE SAME DEER AT 15 MONTHS.—
Foxy brown to golden; ears dusky, edged light, white inside,
fringed snow white; white on top lip, chin, down neck and chest,
under belly, thighs and tail, and on target; bright ginger on tail,
around target and on demarcation line along sides and down neck.

# Measurements and Weights
## (Average Adult)

|  | Indian | Reeves | I/R Cross |
|---|---|---|---|
| Height at shoulder (buck) | 22–23 in. | 17–18 in. | 19–20 in. |
| Height at shoulder (doe) | 18–20 in. | 15–16 in. | 17–18 in. |
| Average clean weight (buck) | 30 lb. | 25 lb. | 26–28 lb. |
| Average clean weight (doe) | 25 lb. | 23 lb. | 23–25 lb. |

G. Kenneth Whitehead
*The Deer of Great Britain and Ireland*

### MEASUREMENTS OF DOE FOUND DEAD ON ROAD, APRIL 1961

Height at shoulder 20 in.
Length from shoulder to base of tail 23 in.
Back leg 14 in.
Head length 7½ in.
Tail 5 in.

### YOUNG DOE FOUND DEAD IN GARDEN, JANUARY 1966

Height at shoulder 19 in.
Length nose tip to base of tail 33 in.
Front leg 11½ in.
Back leg 12½ in.
Head length 7 in.

Ear length 3¼ in. width 2 in.
Neck 5 in.

## FAWN FOUND DEAD. ESTIMATED AGE 1–2 WEEKS. JANUARY 1959

Height at shoulder 11¼ in.
Length nose tip to base of tail 15 in.
Front leg 7¼ in.
Back leg 10 in.
Head length 4½ in.
Tail 2½ in.

# Antlers

'Length of antlers: Reeves 2½–3 in., Indian 3½–5 in.'

G. Kenneth Whitehead
*The Deer of Great Britain and Ireland*

Only the buck carries antlers. These are simple: a short brow tine (developed in the second year) and an unbranched beam. The antlers curve backward converging slightly. They are supported on long hairy pedicles which extend down either side of the forehead forming facial ridges defined on the inner side by dark lines.

In the deer of the garden, length of antlers from sighting: yearling about 1 in.; in the adult buck from 3–5½ in.

In hard horn the colour is pale fawn; in velvet, in mature buck at first blue grey, turning to brownish as velvet shrinks; in young buck, brown.

### CASTING OF ANTLERS IN RELATION TO RUT

| DATE OF RUT | DATE OF CASTING |
|---|---|
| 11–14 July 1966 | 6 August 1966 |
| 2–8 April 1967 | 13 June 1967 |
| 7–8 June 1968 | 27 June 1968 |

## OBSERVATIONS ON BUCK. ANTLERS CAST JUNE 13

| | |
|---|---|
| 23 June | Antlers about $\frac{1}{2}$ in. |
| 3 July | Antlers approximately $1\frac{1}{2}$ in.; velvet blue grey. |
| 26 July | Antlers about 4 in.; velvet brownish, grey at points. |
| 3 August | Antlers approximately 5 in. |
| 5 August | No apparent change. |
| 11 August | No apparent change. |
| 19 August | Velvet showing shrinkage, particularly on brow tines. |
| 24 August | Velvet thinner; brow tines cleaning. |
| 1 September | Velvet showing further peeling. |
| 6 September | Points now clean. |
| 8 September | Velvet only on lower half of antlers; left antler cleaner than right and more sharply curved at point; this one damaged last season while soft. (12 weeks, 3 days from casting.) |

# Teeth

Buck has extended canines forming tusks about $\frac{3}{4}$ in. long in upper jaw.

$$\text{Dental Formula} \quad \frac{0. \quad 1. \quad 3. \quad 3.}{3. \quad 1. \quad 3. \quad 3.}$$

# Scent Glands

Two frontal between facial ribs; two suborbital below the eyes; used by buck to anoint saplings, in communication with does, and to mark out territory; scent also set on food and droppings.

# Tracks

Slots have uneven cleaves. In average adult the foot measures about $\frac{3}{4}$ in. at the heel; in fawn 10 days old, 11 mm. Cleaves splayed in aging deer and when leaping or running at speed. Step, adult, a little under 1 ft. at walking pace; stride, about 20 in.; leaping tracks, up to 9 ft. apart. Step, fawn age about 1 month, at walking pace variable, from 6–8 in.; stride; from 13–15 in.

# Droppings

Size and shape variable; usually ovoid, pointed at one end, occasionally adherent; up to ½ in. in length.

# Voice

The bark of muntjac, buck and doe, is a raucous and somewhat eerie call. Loud and repetitive, it can be heard over a considerable distance and the deer often continues to bark for a long time. It sometimes signifies alarm, and is used in communication among deer; it is heard during the rut, when the doe also gives a high pitched squealing call; a sound reminiscent of muted castanets is sometimes made by running deer. I have heard it from a buck chasing off a younger buck from his territory; the fawn has a shrill yapping bark, occasionally alternating with clear piping calls.

# Food Habitats

Woodland and other terrain containing plenty of low cover and herbage; gardens colonised if semi-wild, with hedges and thickets; coniferous shelter appreciated, as yew with low boughs forming canopy; holly and evergreens in general, attractive in winter.

# General Habits

Diurnal and nocturnal; most active from sunset onward to early morning; feeding at intervals through the night; some wandering by day, but usually lying-up in cover; coming out to feed occasionally and returning to lair to ruminate. Muntjac generally live in family parties; young bucks driven out of territory by reigning buck when over a year old, or younger if they show territorial ambitions; young does remain to varying ages, but may sometimes be driven out by reigning doe when new fawn is expected.

# FOOD

**NATURAL DIET**

Wild herbage including:
    Buttercup spp.
    Hogweed *(Heraculeum sphondylium)*
    Dandelion *(Taraxacum officinale)*
    Ivy *(Hedera helix)*
    Dock *(Rumex obtusifolium)*
    Grass spp.
    Holly *(Ilex aquafolium)*
Fungi spp. including:
    *polyporus sulphereus*
Wild fruit and berries including:
    Crabs
    Rose hips
    Rowan berries
    Sweet chestnuts
    Horse chestnuts
    Acorns

**FOOD SUPPLIED
AND ACCEPTED**

Apples
Pears
Peanuts
Acorns
Sweet chestnuts
Horse chestnuts
Walnuts

**FOOD OFFERED
BUT REFUSED**

Carrots
Turnips
Parsnips
Celery
Brown bread
Oats
Flaked maize
Sultanas
Potatoes (old and new)
Green peas
Beans
Bananas
Raspberries
Gooseberries
Tinned pineapple
Tinned peaches
(No processed or
cooked food taken)

# Temperament

Shy and secretive; the deer prefer to travel in cover where possible; they are extremely timid, and wary of man; not suited to captivity.

# Relations With Man

Muntjac do little harm to man's interests; their chief diet is wild herbage; browsing of tree foliage occasional and scattered, leaves taken sparingly; I have not found any instances of bark stripping or of muntjac damaging root crops or brassicas; accusation of deer damaging sprouts investigated and found to be caused by rabbits: many rabbit tracks in soft ground surrounding plants; no slots of deer in immediate area.

# Rut

There is no fixed season for rutting; this may occur in almost any month; buck shows special interest in doe shortly before the birth of her fawn, and mating takes place soon after; during the rut spells of barking are heard and nuptial chase is characteristic, with racing paths formed among herbage; the rut generally lasts over several days to a week; gestation period 7–8½ months.

| RUT:<br>Periods of barking<br>during several nights | RUT:<br>Periods of barking<br>and new paths<br>formed where<br>buck has chased doe | GESTATION PERIOD |
|---|---|---|
| 14–16 APRIL 1963 | | |
| — | | |
| 10–13 APRIL 1964 | | |
| 27–30 JULY 1964 | | |
| — | | |
| 8–10 DECEMBER 1965 | | |
| | 11–14 JULY 1966 | 37 weeks<br>Approx. 8½ months |
| 2–8 APRIL 1967 | | 29 weeks<br>Approx. 7 months |
| — | | — |
| 6 NOVEMBER 1967 | | 29 weeks<br>Approx. 7 months |
| 15–16 APRIL 1968 | | 32 weeks<br>Approx. 7½ months |
| | 7–10 JUNE 1968 | 28 weeks<br>Approx. 7 months |

# REPRODUCTION

| PERIOD OF TIME BETWEEN RUT AND FIRST SIGHTING OF FAWN | BIRTH OF FAWN (Approx.) | FAWN SIGHTING AND FINDING OF SMALL SLOTS |
|---|---|---|
| 33 weeks App. 8 months | | Small slots found 3 Dec. 63 |
| — | | Fawn seen 4 Oct. 64 Approx. age 3 months |
| 37 weeks App. 9 months | | Small slots found 27 Dec. 64 |
| 38 weeks App. 9½ months | | *Spotted fawn seen 19 Apl. 65 †Approx. age 2 weeks |
| — | | *Spotted fawn seen 28 Dec. 65 †Approx. age 3 weeks |
| 33 weeks App. 8 months | | Spotted fawn seen 27 July 66 †Approx. age 3 weeks |

*29–30 MARCH 1967

*5 NOVEMBER 1967

14–15 APRIL 1968

*26 MAY 1968

1 DECEMBER 1968

*20 DECEMBER 1968

†Age estimated by date of rut, which usually follows

*By the same doe     birth of fawn

139

# Index